The Art of Therapy & The Therapy of Art

by

Anna S. Krayn, PH.D

Crane Publishing
Paramus, New Jersey

Publisher: Yakov M. Krayn
Copy Editor: Nama Sendral
Cover and Text Design: Tatiana Sindalovskaia
Photographs: Ilya Spektor

THE ART OF THERAPY & THE THERAPY OF ART
copyright © 1998 by Anna S. Krayn.
Published by Crane Publishing

Library of Congress Cataloging-in-Publication Data

Krayn, Anna S.
      The Art of Therapy and Therapy of Art / Anna S. Krayn
      p. cm.
      includes bibliographical references and index

      ISBN 0-9665870-0-6
      first edition

      1 psychotherapy. 2 psychology. 3 mental illness-diagnoses. 4 art. 5 symbolism (psychol-
      ogy). 6 visual perception. I title.

Printed in the United States of America
0 9 8 7 6 5 4 3 2 1

Contents

Book Team

Regina Spector

Marina Shikhman

Maria Bardash

Alla Lipetsker

Anna S. Krayn, Ph.D

Preface

In front of you is the result of seventeen years of experience with art therapy. It contains a collection of patients' art work, together with analyses of their drawings, real life case studies, and summaries of research. It also demonstrates and celebrates human fantasies and imagination.

Please, do not read it if you know everything about yourself. Do not look through it if you understand your children easily. Do not even open this book if you are not curious about human psychology or human personality. And certainly, if you think that a person's picture mostly show the drawing skills of the artist, this book is not for you.

But… If art is meaningful to you; if you want to know more about your children; if your own, as well as other peoples, feelings are interesting to you – open this book and study it. It is likely that here you will find more questions than answers, that your interpretation of pictures will be different, and that you will not receive concrete recommendations or solutions. This book is not a manual.

There already exists a rich body of literature on art therapy for professionals. However, I believe that this book adds something new to the existing literature. Not only it allows for understanding of the utility of art therapy, as well as providing the inside look at the dynamics of the art treatment. This book could be, also, used as a diagnostic guide for professionals and as a source of information for parents and for those who are interested in learning about human personality. In any case, the book was written not only for professionals, but also for anyone who is interested in psychology, social works and art. The reader will find here real life stories, illustrated by the main characters; pictures, which were drawn by people at different stages of their life; colors expressing the feelings of the people who use them; and much more. Book references will help you identify your own pictures, your children or your students'. Parents will see some ideas about their children emotional stages and problems; teachers will get help recognizing some particular problems in a class, therapists can use it as a guide for both diagnostic and treatment processes.

Introducing the book, I would like to say a few things about the people who helped me create it. This book is a team effort. All of us devoted as much knowledge, talent, intelligence and personality as we could. Let me introduce four wonderful people who made this publication possible.

Regina Spector – eighteen-year-old musician, composer, singer, poet, writer. Is that enough? For most people it is, but not for Regina. Her extraordinary talent helped rework the clinical cases into short stories. Her writing, as well as her ability to understand the feelings and ideas of others, greatly enhanced this book.

Marina Shikhman -twenty-two-year-old psychologist and artist. I am not sure that she has a skin. She easily picks up emotions, feels them through open nerve; deeply analyzes, and does it all so naturally that you think she was created especially for this. She is truly the best person to study people's moods and feelings.

Maria Bardash – twenty-four-year-old psychologist-in-training. She is my lovely niece, who decided to dedicate her professional life to psychology. I am extremely proud of her intelligence, knowledge, responsibility, and understanding of human psychology. Her insight is present throughout the whole book.

Alla Lipetsker – I have known her since her childhood. At the age of eight, she was bright and always ready to listen for hours upon hours to real life stories. Even at that young age, her comments were amazing, always logical, intelligent, and mature. She is now seventeen, looking for a future career. It is not clear what field she will choose, but her great sense of humor, sensitivity, and ability to analyze and propose solutions will benefit any profession she chooses. Her contribution to the book is both valuable and intriguing.

* * *

Oh, and now about myself. These are my portraits. Only one of them made by a professional artist. The two others are my patients' artistic works and I think they show much more of my personality. I was born in 1954 in Saint Petersburg, Russia, graduated from Saint Petersburg University in 1976, and for thirteen years lectured on sociology and psychology as a university professor. In 1981 I created a psychotherapy program for artists, actors, musicians, and writers. In 1986 defending my Ph.D. dissertation, which summarized my experience with creative people, I realized that the great power of art therapy is one of my favorite approaches. For the last eight years since graduating from Wurzweiler School of Social Work, I have practiced as a psychotherapist in New York and New Jersey.

I would like to take this opportunity to thank Rosa Roberts, Carol Salmanson, and Roni Berger, whose dedication helped me through very difficult times in my life, and the wonderful teachers and parents of Abraham Joshua Heschel School – whose support gave my family and me the unique opportunity to acculturate in a new country. Many thanks to Ilya Spektor, who provided the great technical support in the reproduction of the pictures into slides.

Dear reader! This book is full of pictures. No professional artist drew them. However, these pictures talk about human life, feelings and emotions so clearly, that they became art creations. Look at these pictures and relate to the feelings of those who drew them. I hope that this book will be helpful for you in many areas of your private and professional life.

Introduction

Traditionally, art therapy was used as a therapy for retarded and mentally disabled people who had difficulties with verbal expression of their feelings. Experience shows that art therapy can be an equally successful approach with people of average and high intelligence. For example, art therapy, is effectively used with an immigrant population facing problems with acculturation and adjustment. It is almost impossible for them to express their feelings in an unknown language, to talk directly about their own cultural values, and to discuss their difficulties and problems.

Art therapy helps people to get in touch with their feelings in two ways. First, it foster the expression of feelings and emotions through paintings, using paints, brushes, and canvas. Secondly, it allows people to discuss, explore, and investigate those feelings and emotions, in a less direct and therefore safer manner. Art therapy techniques let people talk more openly and express their feelings through colors and figures in their pictures. Exploration of their anxiety, anger, frustration and weaknesses leads to better understanding of themselves. When positive feelings appear in pictures, people are given a great opportunity to recognize and acknowledge them. Together with the therapist, they can discuss new events, feelings and thoughts, utilizing new insights that they gained through art therapy.

Art therapy can also be used during group and family therapy as a way to increase communication among the participants as they discuss their artwork. Through art therapy, both children and their parents grow closer, learning from their art work about each other's feelings and emotions. Art therapy allows a patient and a therapist to visualize the dynamics of the treatment process. It also helps people to move from feelings of frustration and anger toward themselves and others, to confidence and satisfaction.

For the therapist who uses art therapy, patient's pictures are a great source of information. Combinations of colors, a manner of painting, and pictorial elements , could be expressions of several disorders: depression, anxiety, adjustment, and posttraumatic disorders. By examining the drawings, patients and therapists can learn a lot about patients' feelings, strengths and weaknesses that are often hidden from the patients own awareness.

The author has had seventeen years of experience working with this approach with individuals, families, and groups from various cultural backgrounds. Those who participated in group and individual art treatment solved their problems much easily than those who did not utilize art therapy. These participants were able to maintain their cultural values and develop a positive personal identity. They were able to build and renew family relationships based on their newly acquired communication skills.

The Art of Therapy and Therapy of Art is conceived as the first book in a series about application of art therapy with various populations. It is also a research-based guide to interpretation and exploration of people's work.

Eight years ago my clinical supervisor Rosa Roberts, office manager Carol Salmonson, and I as a therapist discussed a case in need of both, administrative and clinical decisions.

"Do you realize" said Rosa "that if we publish any of our cases, chances are people will never believe them to be true?"

"I am not even the therapist, and I know this from all the years of administrative work in this office." Carol answered.

At that moment I decided that this is exactly what I would do. After all, most of these cases are better than fiction. Each one has an intricate and unique story. Most are hard to believe.

In order to protect patient confidentiality all names and minor details were changed. All the pictures are real, and all the patients gave their permission for publishing their artistic work. Here they are.

Story 1   Liza and Michael
Story 2   Maria
Story 3   Greg
Story 4   Daniel
Story 5   Jennifer
Story 6   Vera
Story 7   Alex

Locating referenced exhibits

Exhibits may come out of order - vertical exhibits fillow horizontal ones on separate pages. Please use exhibit number as referenced to locate exhibits.

Chapter I

Seven Stories

Chapter 1

Lisa & Michael

I

"My husband is an alcoholic", she said. She was petting the sleeping child. She had taken off her glasses and let down her long brown hair from the tight ponytail. "My husband is an alcoholic, that is his designated title. It is sad that your daddy is sick. Many people don't know that he is an alcoholic, they think he's a plumber, and he is, in addition to drinking… he plumbs." At this time she swept her hand over the child's forehead.

"He loves you, and me, and your older sister. We had to leave, you know. Those last couple of years, they were so hard. Now that I look back at it, I don't know how we made it this far. I was the only one working, and he was on unemployment. I worked as a clerk, and all the women would whisper about our family 'condition'. People are like that, sometimes. People will smile at you and say, 'Hello', and then turn to each other with a grand fake pity in their eyes. I wish I could tell you it will be different here, but in that respect people are the same everywhere."

The little girl yawned and turned on her side to face the wall. The mother continued even more quietly than before. "Before we left Russia, there was a kind of unspoken excitement between me and your father. Like we could just pack, and all our problems would stay behind. Like the ocean would separate us from our past forever."

At this point she got up and tiptoed over to the lit kitchen. With mechanical, almost robotic moves, she opened the refrigerator. The little light inside didn't go on, it had burnt out more than two weeks ago. Like the so many other malfunctioning things in the apartment, the light was being ignored.

"But when we came here, it was too real. It was just another reality, only this time we were in desperate need of subtitles. Your father began drinking, and I began learning English. I began to understand the commercials on television, and your father was still just drinking. Drinking and complaining about the 'damn language not going into his head!'" Even though there was no light in the refrigerator, she knew exactly where things were. She took out the cheese and the bread and the pickles and the plate and the cup. She put them on the table. She made herself a sandwich.

As she quietly walked back into the room with the food, her voice automatically lowered. "It isn't right of me to take up your time like this, while you are resting. I'm always rambling on and on, like a terrible fly that buzzes in you ear. But there is never any time during the day. And I get so tired of English. After I come back from work, it lingers in my mouth, like an unpleasant aftertaste. My mouth always hurts, as if it has been full of thumbtacks… the office is full of thumbtacks, and staples, and paper clips."

A crumb fell into the girl's bed. "Oh, I am so clumsy these days! I swear I will make a terrible mess for you. So you see, you will have to forgive your mother for her messes and ramblings. It is nice to talk to someone in Russian, and it is nice to hear your own voice bouncing off the walls.

"Liza?… Liza… Liza, what are you doing still up? You need to go to bed, you need to get some sleep!" The course male voice came from the dark bedroom.

"Michael, I just wanted to get a bite, I will go… I will go to bed soon.""Have a bite? Are you insane? What is it, two in the morning by now?"

"I'm brushing my teeth and coming right to bed. Why are you getting up? Don't get up."

"I just want to get a drink."

Exhibit 1.1.1

Exhibit 1.1.2

Exhibit 1.1.3

Chapter 1

"No, please don't."

"Not that kind of a drink. I might as well, I am up."

"Well alright, but don't be too long."

He walked slowly into the light of the corridor. And she walked past him into the bedroom. They gave each other a ritual, husband-wife glance, the kind that says everything and nothing at the same time. He poured himself a cold glass of water from the sink, and walked over to the little girl's bed. He was not an easy talker like his wife. He only said one thing, but in it there were all his feelings, all his fears. He said, "Tomorrow is the appointment." He said this and then sat in the dark for a long time.

II

Many months had passed since that night. The first uncomfortable moments of therapy, the first strokes of the paintbrush over canvas, seemed a forever ago. All the arguments of "I am not a child anymore! How do you expect me to paint, when I can't even speak my thoughts?" had come and gone, and only a couple of days ago Michael and Liza painted their last picture, together. It was their idea to end this way.

In the early stages of therapy, Michael's art reflected his view of the world around him and the way he functioned within that world (exhibit 1.1.1). He saw that world as chaotic, and himself as the organized man trapped amongst the disorder. The portrait showed the self-centered, even selfish, side of Michael, who battled the outside pressure by retracting further into his thoughts.

Liza's early picture (1.1.2) also depicts chaos, but unlike her husband, she is one with the spinning world. Swept up by the raging tornado in her picture, she seems helpless and alone. Liza feels as though she cannot create a wall around herself, as her husband has done. There is much sadness, depression and exhaustion in this picture.

As the therapy continues the pictures change. Michael's next stage of therapy is reflected in his art by many new concepts in his life (1.1.3). He begins to understand that his attempt at isolation is just a facade, and that the life within him is just as chaotic as the one outside. Liza, in her next phase, depicts the utter loneliness she is experiencing (1.1.4). Her nostalgia for the snow of Russia creates a powerful image.

One of the last pictures was created by the couple together (1.1.5). It is a mixture of idealism and nostalgia as well as optimism for the future. Each spouse felt that working together was a possibility, and each chose a task. Michael painted the landscape, and Liza painted the details. The marriage was now more of a partnership, rather than a competition. It took a long time, but slowly the chaos subsided.

Yet they did not live happily ever after, even though they were much happier. The problems did not miraculously vanish into a forgotten past. Life was still full of complications, and they were still working hard to solve the everyday malfunctions that are present in everyone's life. Someone did, however, replace that burnt out light bulb in the refrigerator, and the late night confessions in the children's room did become rare, making room for the new discussions, the ones at the dinner table.

Exhibit 1.1.4

Exhibit 1.1.5

Chapter 1

Clinical information:

LIZA

Twenty-six-year-old white female.
Thin, nice looking, appropriately dressed.

Axis   I: Major Depressive Disorder,- 296.23
Axis II: None
Axis III: None
Axis IV: Stressor – immigration, relationships with the husband
Axis V: GAF at the beginning of treatment = 45, GAF at discharge = 98

Treatment approaches:
Art therapy;
Psychoanalysis;
Family therapy;
Cognitive – behavioral approach.

Duration of treatment:
Twenty-nine sessions.

MICHAEL

Twenty-nine-year-old white male.
Overweight, unshaven, messily dressed

Axis   I: Alcohol-Induced Mood Disorder,- 291.8
Axis II: None
Axis III: None
Axis IV: Stressor – adjustment, alcohol dependency.
Axis V: GAF at the beginning of treatment = 34. GAF at discharge = 83

Treatment approaches:
Art therapy;
Psychoanalysis;
Family therapy;
Cognitive – behavioral approach.

Duration of treatment:
Twenty eight sessions.

Chapter 1

Maria

I

She sat by the window of her apartment drinking yet another cup of tea. Moscow was staring back at her from beyond the frosty windowpanes. Any minute now a friend would call on her, and they would go for a walk and talk about something new or something old. They would just talk in general and everything would be good. "Any minute now!" she wished, but everything just stood idly by as she kept drinking her tea.

This time it was New York that was staring back at Maria, and she knew better than to wish for an old friend on this cold late afternoon. New York looked even uglier and dirtier when transposed onto the reflection of the pretty Russian teenager. Maria slowly met her own gaze in the dusty window, surveyed it in disgust for a moment, and then put the empty cup on the kitchen table and left the room.

Maria walked through the dark corridor and into her room. She softly closed the door behind herself, and turned on the radio. "See store for details…" she heard the announcer say. The soft female voice went on to say many other things, in a cooing, almost singing tone. Maria did not understand a lot of what was said, but she did not mind. The only thoughts crossing her mind as she sat on the floor rug were sad regrets at the course and vulgar sound of her own voice when she spoke English. She felt incapable, almost infantile, whenever she tried to express her ideas, so she stopped. Maria stopped talking to her American peers and only socialized with a group of Russian teenagers.

"These friends of yours, they are rude and undisciplined what do you see in them?" her mother would inquire.

"I like them, mama, and they like me. You just hate me being happy! You want me to sit alone in my room all day?" Maria would yell back. She would cry, for she really did not like them at all. The only thing these friends and she had in common was that they were Russian. She did not trust the girls, and the guys were only after one thing. One thing so, she stopped feeling. Night after night they would meet and morning after morning she would wake up and feel guilty. As if her body was dirty, and the tiles in the bathroom were too white. Everything was too white next to her.

Maria read books; she would skim the familiar pages with her fingers and mouth the familiar Russian words slowly, as to prolong the pleasure. She would read in her world, and then close the tattered cover and leave it behind, reluctantly. The books she read, the art she saw, were intimate parts of her soul. No one knew them, and so, no one could violate them. She never talked about her interests with the Russian girl friends, it was always movies, or shopping, or boys. Yes, the boys who when they got together preferred not to speak at all. The boys relied mostly on physical communication alone. Maria pressed the snooze button on her radio and went to sleep. She did not dream.

When she awoke the next morning she found herself still fully dressed from the night before. She remembered that she had a couple of tests, and some homework to make up, from her absences. For weeks she had done barely any work. But it was all right; she was absent much of the time, all of it legal, of course, in the eyes of the Board of Education. "Signed by mommy!" she bitterly recalled. By now her mother's signature was so well perfected that she lapsed into it occasionally, while doodling in her notebook, or on test papers. "I deserve a holiday…" And with these thoughts she tiptoed to the bathroom.

The routine of Maria's "holiday" days was little short of a perfect strategy. She would leave her house early in the morning, supplied with a back pack and lunch money. She would then walk to the park and sit on a bench and stare at the people rushing for work. She would

Chapter 1

wait until at least two babysitters with little carriages appeared, then she would take her time and walk back to her apartment. Everybody would have gone to work, and she would watch the talk shows in peace and quiet. At about fifteen minutes to one she would take the stairs down to the lobby and miss her mother, who came home to eat lunch every day, at one. She would then light up a cigarette and walk the streets once more. It usually took about three cigarettes with short breaks in between until her mother had gone again, and Maria would return and spend the next few hours watching the soap opera people live their soap opera lives. She knew them all by name, them and their ex husbands, and brothers, and postal workers.

Katya would drop by, sometimes, around four o'clock, and tell Maria about the new guy she met, and last night, and other life pleasantries. Maria would listen and then Katya would leave. Then it was back to the box for some comedies. Sometimes she would doze off to the continuous laugh tracks. "They are so rhythmical, like the ocean or something." It would be lovely. Lovely...

Soon the tired family members would begin to flow back into the apartment. The walls would get tighter, and the ceiling would seem to almost lower itself from its usual height. Everybody would be too tired to speak, to tired to smile. "How was school?" "Did you do your work?" "Why are you always in front of the television when I come home?" "Why this?" "Why that?" Why... When ... Who...The interrogation would slowly mound together from every direction. "Like a huge snow ball," Maria imagined. They never seemed too tired to yell at her.

Maria put on jeans and a shirt and left her house. It was evening now, and all the apartments were spilling yellow light onto the sidewalks. "You are so lucky" her friends always said, "your family lets you wear anything you want, go anywhere. They are so cool!" "They say they don't want any trouble." Maria would explain. To herself she thought, "They don't care."

In the beginning, her mother and father would confront her, but they were worried that the neighbors would hear. They liked to have things quiet, and even when they argued amongst themselves, her parents closed the door and attempted what sounded like a loud whisper. Now it dwindled down to questions, and even those needed no answers from Maria. "Indeed, I am lucky."

Soon, however, matters got truly worse. One day, Maria's mom took an early lunch and found her vegetating by the television. Another time her father came early from work and found her hanging out with a bunch of her Russian friends in the apartment. The floor was carpeted with beer and vine bottles, courtesy of her friends. Soon enough the teachers began calling, and even the principal scheduled an appointment for Maria and her parents at his office. The secretive family was in shock. Maria was numb. The friends were shallow. The soap opera people, however, kept on living their soap opera lives, some got killed off in tragic accidents, and others found their long lost brother on the mother's side, twice removed. Somehow, something had to change.

II

A teenage girl sits in a psychotherapist's office. Her family has insisted upon her being there because they can no longer handle her rebellious behavior. A family in which it was never proper to talk about problems or troubling ideas has decided that she should pour her soul out to a stranger with a medical degree. A family in whose eyes she has hit rock bottom wants her to reclaim her lost reputation and innocence, and thus, she sits in a psychotherapist's office.

Maria, an immigrant from Russia, is at this doctor's office as the last resort. She has been cutting school, failing tests, talking back to her parents at home and in public, and as her family put it, "not being herself". The objective of the therapist, however, consists of much more than reconstructing the patient's life to its previous state. The therapist must learn to understand this patient and her problems, and find out what was wrong within her life previously, why it is

Exhibit 1.2.2

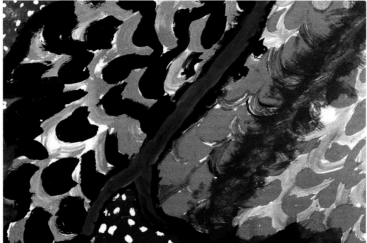

Exhibit 1.2.1

Chapter 1

emerging now, and how it should be dealt with before moving on.

In order to be effective, the therapist must achieve a level of trust and communication with the patient. In Maria's case this is rather complex since she has little or no experience discussing issues openly in her family. Her eyes are fixed on the walls, she is defensive, and her body is tense, as if striving to make herself as small and impenetrable as possible. Maria is not about to speak her personal problems aloud, nor is she prepared to believe that the therapist can, realistically, help. And so she sits across from the doctor, and, like in an old cowboy movie, she gets ready to draw.

When she is given a clean canvas and a set of paints, however, her expression changes from frustration, to confusion. She laughs and says that she is not a child, and that colors will not repair her problems. She is not reluctant to try it, though, especially since she has the option of not to speaking. As she begins to draw with the first few uneasy strokes, she is still self-conscious, but the presence of the therapist soon becomes comfortable. Slowly all the emotions flow out and onto the canvas as a hurricane of feelings and ideas fills the office. There are no judges, no scores, and no limits freedom at last.

After she completes the first painting, a look of contentment comes over the girl's face. The therapist gently explains the significance of this first step to her. Now the therapist is accepted as help, and not shut out as just another critic. Maria goes on to explain what she was trying to draw, not even realizing that she is describing her own emotions. The paintings create a shield to shelter Maria from feeling violated, while still allowing for her to talk about private matters.

In one of Maria's first paintings (exhibit 1.2.1), dark colors, reds and blacks, create the atmosphere of pain. She says, "I was brought here like a baggage item, without consent." The canvas is still there beneath her hands, a testimony to all her troubles, but soon the canvas becomes more of a communication device, rather than a shield.

In Maria's second stage of therapy (exhibit 1.2.2), a new style of painting emerges. It is less abstract, and more symbolic, than in her previous work. Maria knows her heart is broken. The black half of the heart is the New York around her, the red half is her passionate love for the culture she has left behind. The glimpses of blue represent, both, her attempt at happiness and its scarcity.

Later on (exhibit 1.2.3), Maria begins to further understand her own duality. The snake-like roads painted yellow and black (a color combination often associated with suicidal tendencies) seem to lead towards something concrete, but not necessarily positive. The other half of the picture depicts a tall and intimidating. New York, her future home. The repetitive skyscrapers stand atop uncertainty. There is water and a red pedestal serving as the foundation in this heavy city. Maria, however, does see some positive aspects in this portrayal. Even though there is a great tension between her two worlds, Maria is finally feeling again. The separation between these two worlds is sharp, but so are the accompanying emotions. Even the dreary New York takes on a brighter perspective next to the chaotic alternative.

During the last stages of Maria's therapy she draws a picture still reflecting the uncertainty of her life (exhibit1.2.4). While painting this picture, Maria makes a technical mistake, and drips the yellow paint from the sun, lower onto the canvas. She decided to keep it, saying, "The sun is already rising, but I am crying from the pain…"

It is common for a patient to make a technical mistake, and then see the hidden meaning behind it. Art therapy helps Maria, and many others, become more introspective. By seeing their own thoughts and feelings on the canvas before her, the patients learn how to locate and deal with problems.

Exhibit 1.2.3

Exhibit 1.2.4

Chapter 1

Clinical information:

MARIA

Fifteen-year-old white female.
Average weight, hopeless-looking, appropriately dressed.

Axis   I: Major Depressive Disorder,-296.33
Axis II: None
Axis III: None
Axis IV: Stressor – immigration.
Axis V: GAF at the beginning of treatment = 45; GAF at discharge = 93

Treatment approaches:
Art therapy;
Family therapy;
Psychoanalysis;
Cognitive – behavior approach.

Duration of treatment:
Forty-nine sessions.

Chapter 1

Greg

I

It glowed blue. It glowed strong. It proudly announced its name: "Toyota Eclipse". Two doors, six cylinders, XXX horsepower, and eleven black stripes on the fabric of the back seat. The climax of Greg's eight- year- old life had just presented itself. All its glory and power now stood majestically on the road. Greg had witnessed the birth of this steel Venus and now stood paralyzed with amazement. All those who said that technology could not bond a family were just proven wrong. The spectacle held the family members in awe.

In fact, since the appearance of this new family member, things could not have been any better. No more worries of where the money would come from. This single purchase proved that wherever it came from, it finally learned the way to Greg's house. No longer would the kitchen table serve as a forum for financial debates. "Can we afford it?" would no longer be the ever-present question on everybody's mind. The mother stopped cursing that "damned unemployment" because the father was no longer unemployed. The discordant four years since the family had arrived in America were now safe in the past.

That past held great significance in the boy's life. Greg made his earthly appearance into a greedy world, a world that greedily withheld air from his tiny lungs for almost half a year, at which time a compromise was made. The six- month- old Greg had fought hard for his life and left the hospital in his father's arms. In three and a half years, he left his country as well, this time walking alone and holding his father's hand.

When he got to America, however, Greg offered only silence to the English speaking world. He was convinced that this world did not deserve his acknowledgement or attention. More important things, such as observing the family feuds which took center stage in his kitchen, took up most of his time and energy.

Greg never brought a model car to the kindergarten's "show and tell". He never chased his kindergarten "bad guys" while playing "cops and robbers. He never called another preschooler a bad name, and never got in trouble with the teacher. Little Greg simply forbade America to interfere with his life. No English words. No friends. No "thanks you."

Occasionally a six- year-old could be seen knocking on Greg's door. Greg would let him in, cautiously, holding his father's gaze with the corner of his eye. Finally, and to the joy of his parents and friends, Greg joined his peers in games and fun. Within a couple of years his whispers, laughs and yells knew no boundary. Greg became involved with friends and seemed much happier when out of the house.

In the house, however, the yelling continued. A week before his eighth birthday familiar arguments filled the air. But the unemployment could not be blamed on the father any longer, because now his father finally had earned a job.

Now Greg looked at the Eclipse and put on a pair of sunglasses. They protected his eyes from its glowing blue finish. Well, they would anyway, when the sun came out. Confidently his father sat as the conqueror in the front seat. Greg strapped himself securely in the back, and the three of them blew dust in the direction of their old wreck of a car.

The car floated into the intersection. It gracefully obeyed the father's command to stop at the red light. The truck behind it, however, did not. The crashing sound echoed through the impermeable shell of the car. Greg knew that it could not destroy the car's commander. "It's ok," came his father's words, "it's all over now." "It's all over now... it's all over now..."The words filled the air. And then another car jammed into the mass, breaking his father's promise - that worthless promise from a lying father.

The stretcher carried the boy away. The wheel chair carried him around for the next six

Chapter 1

weeks. Confidently the doctors diagnosed no injury in Greg's legs or torso. But something in Greg was desperately trying to prove them wrong. His legs supported all motion, sensation and everything else except his weight. His mind supported everything except his father. Fear was filling in the gaps.

II

Greg walked in to the psychotherapy office holding his mother's hand. Once inside he strategically maneuvered himself to the chair. He maintained as great a distance from his father as his geometric skills would allow. After the initial interview and some coaxing, the parents reluctantly left the room. This left me, Gregory, and a blank canvas. The idea of acrylics, a large canvas and multiple brushes soon got the better of the reluctant artist. Diligently Greg began sketching out what soon became the ground floor for our work.

A large automobile slowly dominated the canvas (exhibit 1.3.1). The feeling he fearfully remembered as he closed his eyes and searched through his memory started to flow out on to the paper. "What are you drawing?" I casually inquired. He shrugged with carelessness.

His brush saturated with black paint, Greg was forcefully drawing a circle. "I hate cars," he informed me as even more black paint started to shape the car's body. "And you know what else," he remarked, "I hate my father." With that he picked up another brush and forcefully colored in the body of his car.

During later therapy sessions Greg's painting indicated both progress and problems. Although his next drawing (exhibit 1.3.2) omitted the frightening black feeling of the car, the atmosphere of danger was not gone from the painting. A large black orb hovers in the air of the painting. Greg's anger and fear flow onto the canvas in dominating, dark strokes. The relationship between Greg and his father can be monitored from the distance of the ball from the car. As the dark sphere moves away from the car, Greg's relationship with his father begins to reconstruct. Greg was learning that his father could , make mistakes as well as accomplish wonderful things. Messages such as "help kill" (exhibit 1.3.3) became "Fix" (exhibit 1.3.4). Greg was moving from the world of extremes to one of adjustments. Yet, the emotional weight still remained in his next painting (exhibit 1.3.5). A large and heavy object hovers over both his head, and the dog's.

At home, little by little, Gregory and his father spent more time together. The final sign of reunion came when the two bought an "easy bake" cake. Greg gleefully asked to bake it himself. Upon receiving approval, Greg went on to prove exactly how easily an "easy bake" recipe went sour. When the batter resembled water more then dough, Greg started to cry; it was evening, so getting another cake was impossible. In Greg's moment of despair his father suddenly announced that they could fix the problem. Choosing careful wording his father clearly established that the mistake was theirs, and that together they could surely correct it. Dumping some extra flour, sugar and baking soda into the mush, they eventually produced a cake and slid it into the oven. "My father," Greg exclaimed to me at the office, "he can solve anything!"

Greg's final therapy visit came on a worm spring day. Positioning the canvass by the window Greg took a look at the outside trees. He let out a decisive sigh and went on to paint his last exhibit (exhibit 1.3.6). Greg's trees bear little resemblance to the evergreen bushes outside my office window. His trees stand for the three members of their family. The evergreen pine, the one different from the others is Greg's mother. He and his father are the same - they are "men."

Exhibit 1.3.1

Exhibit 1.3.2

Exhibit 1.3.3

Exhibit 1.3.4

Exhibit 1.3.5

Exhibit 13.6

Chapter 1

Clinical information:

GREG

Eight-year-old white male.
Average weight, looking upset, appropriately dressed.

Axis   I: Generalized Anxiety Disorder, - 300.02
Axis II: None
Axis III: None
Axis IV: Stressor – relationship with the father.
Axis   V: GAF at the beginning of treatment = 37, GAF at discharge = 92.

Treatment approaches:
Art therapy;
Play therapy;
Family therapy;
Cognitive-behavior approach.

Duration of treatment:
Thirty-three sessions.

Chapter 1

Daniel

I

Daniel sat in the corner of the room and listened to the conversation between the three women.

"He was always this way, always afraid and quiet. I just don't know anymore."

At this point the high pitched voice of his mother was interrupted by the shivering voice of his grandmother. "My poor boy! No matter how much we talk to him, we try to explain there is nothing to be afraid of. Nothing, am I right?"

"You are absolutely right, Mama. Remember when we took him to the park. He cried, a grown boy, afraid of god knows what. I told him that the trees do not bite, and neither do the benches, and....

" Here, again, the grandmother interrupted saying, "And neither do the people!"

Daniel had heard these two voices talking this way, beginning and finishing each other's sentences, comforting each other, millions of times. The only difference was that now they were in an office with a diploma hanging on the wall. They sat on a dark green couch across from the third woman in the room. She was a therapist.

Daniel closed his eyes just as he had numerous times. He saw himself lying on his back and felt wild winds blowing over him. A cold terror swept over him, leaving him covered in goose pimples. Always he had a feeling of something inevitable, something heavy and round, crushing him at any minute. Sometimes Daniel would try to remember what it was like not to feel that way. He could almost remember a time when he was brave, and happy, somewhere in the back of his mind. Yet the harder he tried, the further it seemed to go within his mind, until it seemed like a mere mirage, a ridiculous dream.

The therapist inquired about the father's role in the family.

"Well Michael wants nothing to do with the therapy. Nothing at all. He is very disappointed in his son. Besides he..."

"He believes this is all our doing anyway. He says we babied the boy too much, and now this is the result." As the grandmother said this, she turned red and looked over at Daniel with her worried and watery eyes. "He says that therapy is a feminine thing." The mother added this and looked curiously at the therapist.

II

The therapy began with Daniel drawing pictures. It became rather apparent that his greatest fears lay in round objects, especially oncoming objects. Daniel drew these round objects in swirls over the paper. In his first picture (exhibit 1.4.1), the image is very clouded but also disturbing. In the later pictures, however, the roundness is more apparent and it seems clear that the circle objects are causing some kind of distress to the boy. The climax of his fears is portrayed as a great ball of black and yellow (exhibit 1.4.2). Even though when he was asked to explain his fears Daniel had a standard answer of "I don't know..," the therapist began working on these fear of the approaching round objects. In exhibit 1.4.3, the dog seemed to be crushed by the big approaching ball. Noticing this discomfort from the boy's art, the therapist began rolling little balls toward him, until his fear would subside. She would then increase the size of the ball and slowly begin the process again.

Soon the pictures began to reflect this growing comfort (exhibit 1.4.4), and Daniel began to draw parks with flowers in them. Finally Daniel was able to play with gigantic beach

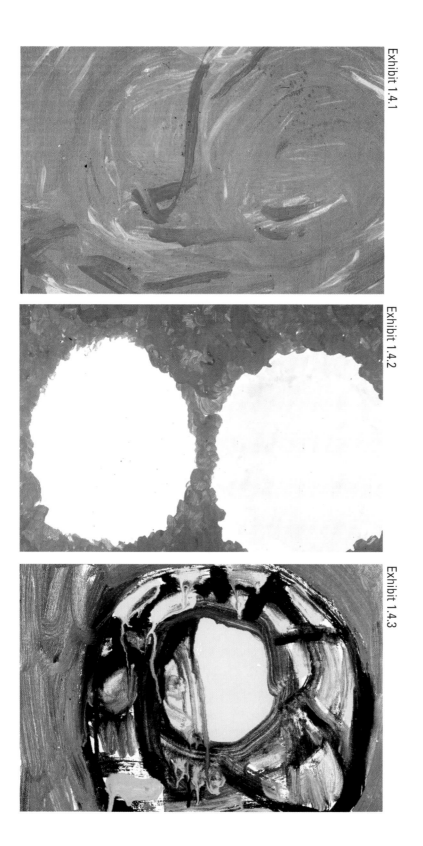

Exhibit 1.4.1

Exhibit 1.4.2

Exhibit 1.4.3

Chapter 1

balls, feeling no anxiety. Both the mother and the grandmother were extremely pleased. Even the father noticed the results and decided to come into the office to meet the therapist. Daniel had been transformed, and the father wanted to personally thank the therapist. During his conversation with the therapist, the father spoke of how brave his little boy was when he was three. He even gave a story as an example.

"Daniel and I went to the park. He was only three. The winds of autumn were blowing unusually hard that day. At first we walked hand in hand, but Daniel wanted to collect some red leaves from the ground, and so I let go and he ran towards the road. Right beyond the road there was a construction site. Suddenly, a giant spool of telephone wire tipped over, and began rolling down the road to where Daniel was collecting the leaves. He tried to run towards me but he tripped and lay flat on his back. He was very lucky for the spool ran right above him. But like I said, my boy was brave, very brave! He got up and didn't even cry. Not one tear!"

At this point the father looked around at all the shocked faces. It was now obvious what kind of trauma caused all of Daniel's fears. Daniel closed his eyes once more and saw himself lying on his back. He heard the wind, but he was no longer afraid. He understood everything.

When the mother finally came to her senses, she asked the father, "Why didn't you say anything before? Why, Michael? What the hell were you thinking, not telling me something like that?"

"I was afraid you would get angry at me for not watching the boy. I figured since no one got hurt, and he didn't cry, and he didn't even say anything, that it didn't matter."

The entire incident was a key, an explanation to the trauma. Even though this story helped answer a lot of questions, Daniel would have gotten better anyway. This revelation was a comforting addition to the already undergone therapy. The art therapy pointed to the fears of round objects and provided an insight into Daniel's subconscious. He could have gone through life without ever knowing the background story and still function because of the answers he provided in his art.

Exhibit 1.4.4

Exhibit 1.4.5

Chapter 1

Clinical information:

DANIEL

Six-year-old white male.
Average weight, looking fearful, appropriately dressed.

Axis I: Posttraumatic Stress Disorder. 309.81
Axis II: None
Axis III: None
Axis IV: Stressor –fear of rolling or moving objects.
Axis V: GAF in the beginning of treatment = 35; GAF at discharge = 87

Treatment approaches:
Art therapy;
Play therapy;
Family therapy;
Psychoanalysis;
Behavioral   approach.

Duration of treatment:
Forty six sessions.

Chapter 1

Jennifer

I

My sister Jen started ninth grade. I guess that gave her a lot to think about. I probably will do a lot of thinking when I go to high school. My father thinks a lot too, even though he is not in high school anymore, but that is because he is the head of the family. He patiently listens to everyone and then goes and thinks things over. One day, he always tells me, I will be making decisions for my family. But until then, I have to talk to him before doing stuff, and so does everyone. Well, at least that's what they are supposed to do, but sometimes they don't.

In high school, Jen made a new friend. A Christian friend. A girl that used to go to that Catholic school in that big brick building. I don't think I've seen her that close with anyone for a while. But I did not think much of it. It was just a little weird seeing a cross on that girl's neck at the dinner table. Not that we are deeply religious or anything like that. It's just that I'm Muslim, nothing out of the ordinary, unless it's a holiday or something really special like that. It was just a little weird because that girl was so into it. And Jen, my sister, she was into her. They'd sit in her room for hours and talk about stuff. They would not let me in, so I didn't know what they were talking about. Now I found out.

So as I was saying, the two of them talked a lot. And I did not know this at the time, but they were talking about Christianity. Jen has always been really nice you know, so I guess she liked that whole "turn the other cheek" thing. So the more they talked, the more Jen fell in love with Christianity. She even started going to church on Sundays. But we did not know, that of course. She needs her privacy, she says. She doesn't have to tell us where she's going anymore, because she is all grown up. My father thought that was pretty reasonable, the privacy thing. She was about to enter college, after all.

Those church visits, though, they became more and more frequent. Once I snooped around her room, like under her mattress and behind the desk drawers. She hid her diary there sometimes, and if she had any other secret things, she'd put them there as well. So one time I found a cross there. But she never wore it when any of us were around. I read something about a church ceremony in her diary, but I did not understand anything really. (Later I found out that she got baptized or what ever they do to make you Christian.) Of course I kept my mouth good and shut about all that stuff. Still, I don't know how she managed to hide all that from mother and father, but I guess she just had her mind set on it. You could see that it was bothering her though, not telling anybody. She was just getting weird all over. One week she'd be into reading books and the next almost ready to burn them. Some weeks she'd be a hermit and then, boom! - she became the most social person in the world.

At first she spent a lot of time at college but then she started coming home more often. That was really nice because she would always talk to Roger and me. Roger is the youngest of the three of us. She told us stories. Stuff about Cain and Abel, and Jesus Christ and other stuff that they were studying in college. She was a really good student too, because she knew so many of them. And after each story she would go on about the "meaning" and "lessons." I guess when you get to college, you can't just enjoy the story - you have to look for something behind it.

One of those times, when she was telling us these stories, our father was standing outside the door. And then he called her over. He said that it was great that she knew so many interesting things. He said that she was a great story teller. But he also wondered why she does not tell us any of the Muslim stories. He said that there were Muslim heroes and deeds that were colorful and interesting.

Chapter 1

Then all hell broke loose. Jen suddenly just blurted lots of stuff out. She said that she was now a Christian, and that we should all be Christians as well. She told him how she got baptized and went to church all the time. But she kept quiet for years because she was afraid to tell anyone. Father got really mad then. He was most upset about was her telling those stories to Roger and me. " Look, Jennifer," he said to her, "you know that I have always respected Judaism, Christianity, Buddhism and anything else. But I am a Muslim, and proud of it. You should be proud of it too. You know this family inside and out, and this is not the right way for us to find out about your new ideas. It has gone too far when you talk to two little boys before your father. Now if Christianity calls you, then we need to deal with that. That may be OK. What you did certainly breaks all limits." Dad thought she was trying to get me and Roger to believe in Christianity before talking to mother and him. Father said that me and Roger are just children and she had no right to use us like that. Then he wanted her to go away. Out of the house. He never wanted to see her again.

He never really threw Jen out, though. Mother convinced him not to. She also convinced him to continue paying for Jen's college. So Jen still lived with us. But it was really different now. Father would not talk to her at all. Mother would speak a little bit while Jen helped her out in the kitchen and stuff. I know they were talking.

Soon after that, Jen started bringing lots of girls home. They'd call each other "sisters" and be really close. They looked like they were really good friends. Hugged each other a lot and stuff like that. Once I even saw them kissing when I was spying in her. But only once. I never saw her do it again. And when I was going through her diary about that time, I came across a picture of a naked lady. I wanted to see it again a little ways later, but it was not there anymore. The page was torn out. That was a real bummer.

But it was a good thing that mother kept Jen talking. Because Jen soon met a man. And he was talking about flowers. Flowers this and flowers that, and flowers are the meaning of life. He told her that she did not belong to anyone. She did not belong to her family, or religion, or even herself. She was just a part of the world, and had to live with that world. He told her of a place where everyone lives in harmony with nature. And where there are brothers and sisters who all understand her. And no one controls any one, just all flowers and harmony and no contact with other people. This man explained that people mess up the nature's harmony, so she had to go away from them. She had to go with him, to their flower place. The amazing thing was, that Jen would idealize this guy. His voice flowed, she'd say, and that he had something that she called "presence." She's hear his voice and feel him near her, a lot of the time. Sometimes, she'd even hear his voice in her sleep.

Well, mother knew right away that Jen was about to join a cult. She suddenly got all cautious. She started telling Jen that it was her choice what she wants to do. She said how much we all love her. She said that Jen could go to the flower world if she chooses, but that she first has to understand herself. If Jen would promise to talk to a therapist, then mother would support her all the way. And then after that mother went and talked to father, and she was in panic. She told him all about the cult and everything. Father started to talk to Jen again, and made sure that she talked to a therapist. And then he and mother talked to the therapist too. Later on even me and Roger went, so it was a whole family thing.

It all worked out, too, because Jen, she never joined that cult. She's back to normal now.

II

Jen casually brushed the canvas with paint at the therapist's office. The colors and shapes she created into the world soon became springboards for conversation. She drew herself

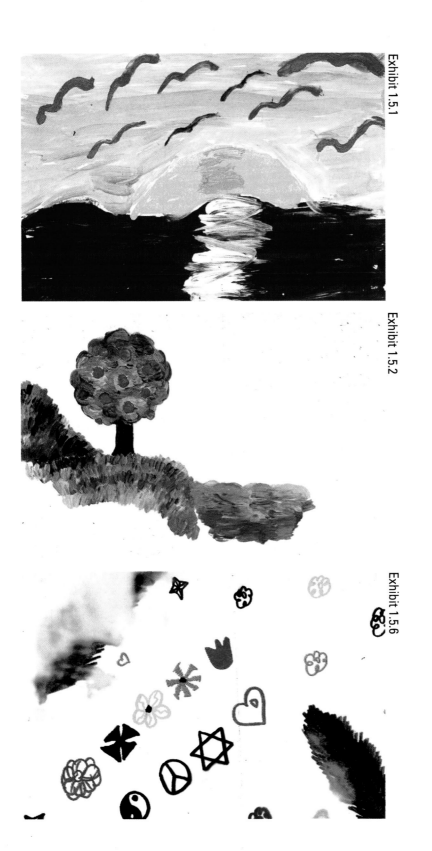

Exhibit 1.5.1

Exhibit 1.5.2

Exhibit 1.5.6

Chapter 1

and nature wondering exactly who she was. Covering the entire canvas with paint (exhibit 1.5.1), Jen left nothing exposed to the air. Going from one extremes to another, the second picture left most of the canvas untouched (exhibit 1.5.2). The picture looks incomplete. The overwhelming emotions battered her mind. As another session was coming to a close, Jen had a hard time leaving the office. "I don't want to go home," she finally articulated. She felt out of place and struggled to discover where she belongs. In her next drawings Jen pondered religion. The religious symbol never appears alone in her art (exhibits 1.5.3 &1.5.4). Always Jen drew something surrounding the cross. Paying careful attention to the now delicate strokes, she drew herself as a cross (1.5.4). Jen was living in a world of anxiety and depression. She felt out of place at home and at school. Even the promising cult no longer appealed to her, and she never entered it. Shortly Jennifer dropped out of college.

One day Jen yet again skeptically entered the office. She took a second setting up the canvas, and almost wordlessly began to paint. A candle and light soon colored the paper (exhibit 1.5.6). Jen's words broke the silence. "I don't know why I'm drawing this," she confessed. But the drawing went on. Together with the therapist they took a closer look at the painting. "I think I am thinking of light," Jen finally suggested.
"What about light?"
"What is light?" she questioned herself. "Is it in a religion? Does it have to be Christian or Muslim?" Jen starting examining her own views. What did she want from life? Riches? Fame? Wealth? What does she want to bring into the world? She wanted to bring something good, she finally decided.

During this stage of therapy Jen's thoughts and discussions started to lead away from who she is alone. Rather, she wondered who she is in the world. Who is she in her family? Who does she want to be? Suddenly a world opened up to her. Being a good person no longer implied being in a certain religion. She started piecing together her life.

During one of the last therapy sessions, Jen's younger brother came bouncing into the office. "We all went to Six Flags last Sunday" he announced. "Dad and Jen and I, we had a bet - on who could eat more ice cream."
"Who won?" the therapist asked.
"Jen. But she can't look at ice cream any more." Jen had finally returned to her family and school.
Jen's final realization came at her last session. She closed her eyes and thought for a second. "It was never about religion in itself, I guess."

Exhibit 1.5.3

Exhibit 1.5.5

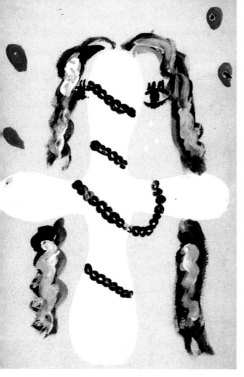

Chapter 1

Clinical information:

JENNIFER
Nineteen-year-old African-American female.
Average weight and heights, careful, gentle and unsure; beautiful face and flowing movement carried a lost look, appropriately dressed.

Axis I: Anxiety Disorder Not otherwise Specified – 300.00
Axis II: None
Axis III: None
Axis IV: Stressor - identity problem and family relationships.
Axis V: GAF at the beginning of treatment = 40, GAF at discharge = 91

Treatment approaches:
Art therapy;
Psychoanalysis;
Family therapy;
Cognitive – behavior approach.

Duration of treatment:
Thirty-one sessions.

Chapter 1

VERA

I

"The Ghettos were filled with Jews. Entire Jewish communities were extracted from their homes, a rather routine surgical procedure. They were part of mass relocation. Your grandmother was eighteen years old at the time. Eighteen… hard to believe." As father said this, his eyes glazed over with a kind of reverent tranquility. "Eighteen, and already dealing with such adverse conditions. Why couldn't you be a little more like her? Why?" As I drew breath to answer, he went on with the story, for this was a rhetorical question. Most of father's questions were rhetorical. "And your grandmother was a saint even at that tender age. She was, and I don't want to see your eyes rolling like that. Have some respect!"

And I did. Come to think of it how could I not have respect for her? I had been spoon fed "Grandma" since childhood. I have heard all the stories, in all their glory, and all the details are forever etched in my memory. When I was little, very little, my fantasy would play upon the adventures of grandma during the war. But soon it became hard to be impressed, it really did. She was everywhere. She invaded my homework, and bedtime stories, dinners, lunches, as well as most breakfasts. When mother died, it got even worse. Dad did not like to talk about her, it was hard for him, and all. But grandma - he would go on about her forever. It was like we were in a contest or something, and I could never win, because she was already dead.

"Are you listening to me, Vera? You were named after her, you know. You have to make me proud, me and your grandmother. That name means a lot, it stands for many great things, so you should get it together. And now that we are in this wonderful country, you have to work twice as hard."

I stopped liking my name when I was twelve. I distinctly remember the day. It was fall and the entire apartment had a damp haze about it. The trees outside, and the people, were swaying slowly. Father came back from work and said, "You are already twelve years old. Do you know what kind of life she was living at twelve? You don't deserve her name! How can you claim it as your own and not be ashamed? Why, when I named you…" Her name - in our house it was her name. A name slipping down my shoulders and off my hips, like an oversized dress during a game of dress-up. I was a clown in that name.

"Our entire family was sitting in that ghetto, like a herd of cows waiting to be processed at the meat plant, except they had no oats to chew on, and no milk to give. And that bitch, she was lying in bed with the Nazi bastard, watching everything through her opera glasses. That bitch!" The bitch was my grandmother's brother's wife. She thought it wise to seduce one of the Nazis overseeing the Ghetto. She would sleep with him, and feed him, and wash his uniform, just in case Germany prevailed. When all the Jews had to begin living in their little designated corner of the world, she got to stay behind. After all, if you are married to a Jew, the most anyone would do is pity you. She and my grandmother's brother had a son. He was seven and got to go between the Ghetto and the outside.

One night she found out that the Ghetto would be liquidated, so being a rational woman she planned everything out. My father put it this way, "The witch thought it improper to be left with a half Jewish child. She gave him some leftovers from her damn meal and told him to spend the night in the Ghetto at his father's."

"But your grandmother, she was a holy woman. She felt something wrong, she had a premonition. She took the little boy by the hand and was walking him towards one of the back passages, to send him home. Suddenly lights and gunshots surrounded them in a hurricane of confusion. She put the boy on her shoulders and ran for her life. The shots were engulfing her, suffo-

Chapter 1

cating her. She ran and ran and never turned around. She ran into the woods and took the boy off her shoulders. He was dead. He took the bullet, which would have killed her. She buried the body and ran deeper and deeper into the woods."

He told me that she became a partisan. That she fell in love with another partisan. That they got married. That they had two children, and that the children were a boy and a girl. That she fought bravely for her country. That I should only pray to be as brave as she is. So I pray. I pray all the time. I pray to never hear him speak of her again. I pray for him to never call to me, "Vera, come to the kitchen, dinner is ready." Because it is always a disappointment when the wrong Vera shows up. The right Vera will never come. Never.

Yet every time father tells the story, it has a dark ending. His face changes as he gets to the last part of the legend. He says, "Your grandmother went on vacation with the two children to the Black Sea. I was the little boy, your Aunt Ellen was the little girl. She always wanted only the best for us. That day, when we were walking on the beach, it was peaceful, and soft. She fainted and all the onlookers just stood and whispered. I stayed with her, and Ellen ran as fast as she could to get help. The next day she was still weak, but she told us to stay home, that she would be back soon. She gave us a sealed letter."

"The sealed letter…" he pauses. He always stops for a minute when he gets to the letter. "She never came back. The police got us. They came in the morning and asked us a bunch of ridiculous things, things that did not matter to anyone. But what she did was monumental. And the letter justified her." I wonder if I could ever be justified. What if I never got to avenge anyone, or write a letter, or die a heroine…?

"She saw that devil woman on the beach. That was the reason she fainted. They said it was a heat stroke, but later we found out the truth. She spoke with her that night, on a bench. She told her about her son's death, she told her about the cruelty, but the witch had no remorse. Your grandmother cried and tried everything to make that cold animal feel. Finally she threatened to tell the authorities about the Nazi, and the planned murder of her family. But the monster just laughed at her. She said that she is an influential person in this town. That she is a doctor. She explained calmly that when she saw the Russians were winning, she turned in her Nazi plaything and got a medal. She said she had the medal in a pretty red box, beneath the mirror. She said she is glad that they all died. That it is too bad more dirty Jews did not. At the end she said it would be your grandmother's word against her. She smiled and said that they would never believe her. She said that a Russian is always more credible than a Jew.

"Your grandmother killed her. She had to…"

My grandmother went to jail. She had to. Soon after she died. The jail had broken her health and her spirit. We saw her only a few times. She apologized. We forgave her. How could we not? She died a heroine." I have to be the heroine now, but there is no place for me to do it. This is Queens, and I'm in school, but I have to be the heroine. Why can't I just change my name?

…

II

In her early pictures, Vera has a rather confused understanding of what she is and what her father desires her to be. She draws joyous objects, such as a Christmas tree, but they irritate her (exhibit 1.6.1) Vera sees everything through the biases and regulations placed upon her by her father. She is lost between her own identity and her grandmother's.

The second picture is drawn with many interactions from the father (exhibit 1.6.2). Vera draws herself when she is older. It seems as if she is growing out of a mass of horrors and pain. She

Exhibit 1.6.1

Exhibit 1.6.2

Chapter 1

said, "I am afraid to think about how I will turn out, but there is always a trail of war behind me. Everything that my father idealized is marked with blood. How can I ever live up to it?" By the next stage of therapy, the father begins to accept some guilt. The line in the picture become clear and defined (exhibit 1.6.3) The boundaries between the truth and reality, idealism and sincerity become more defined, and Vera gains self-confidence and self-worth as the result. In the final and last stage of Vera's therapy, she draws what she titles as a "cute" picture (exhibit 1.6.4). Her relationship with her father has improved tremendously, and she believes that she can now draw in the style of a little girl. Because she has this second chance to live a childhood unpressured or overshadowed by the reputation of her grandmother, she has the ability to accomplish and achieve her own goals.

Exhibit 1.6.3

Exhibit 1.6.4

Chapter 1

Clinical information:

VERA

Thirteen years old white female.
Tall, average weights, looking angry and anxious, appropriate dressed.

Axis I: Anxiety Disorder,-300.00
Parent – Child Problem, - V61.20
Axis II: None
Axis III: None
Axis IV: Stressor – conflicts with the father.
Axis V: GAF at the beginning of treatment = 42; GAF at discharge = 90

Treatment approaches:
Family therapy
Art therapy;   °
Psychoanalysis;

Duration of treatment:
Twenty two sessions.

Chapter 1

Alex

I

I am going to tell you a life story. It is a difficult thing to do. Those people who tell their life stories to any man willing to listen, they are rarely sincere. They use their tales as confessions, they seek sympathy, or admiration, or forgiveness. I, on the other hand, have little to confess. Life has taken me and held me, and thrown me away. I just want to speak.

The war is starting, right? So, I see people everywhere stumbling towards their little train carts. No one has a specific destination; people just flow in sweaty currents. They are all going down, down, down stream. Small, thin, vein like, the streets get flooded with Jews, herds and herds of Jews. It was frightening. It was exciting. Sweat and voices engulfing and devouring that world. What a world!

And my mother is there, too. And my sister is also there. Dad was dead by then, but the three of us were fine. Here and there would be Nazis, a beautiful sight. They had crisp clean uniforms, which looked even more beautiful in contrast with the surrounding rags. They would toss glances, scornful and majestic, at the rest of us. They had guns. Occasionally they would shoot someone. A single cry would be heard, but moments later the mass of voices would resume their wail, and it would be forgotten.

I think they were beautiful because they were so horrible. I saw them in my dreams for years. They would look like crisp icicles, and seem almost frozen and breakable. One of them would always begin to topple over, and if I would not wake up before that moment, the soldier would crash down, in slow motion, and break into thin glass splinters.

"Hold my hand… hold hands, Alex! Nina, hold your brother's hand… Don't look up dear. Do you hear me? Don't look at any soldiers." My mother was not short. I was nine, and tall for my age, but she towered over me as she spoke. "I meant to take that pretty scarf your late uncle gave me three years ago… Hurry up, we have to be quick!" We were out of breath. We were out of everything. "Don't you worry, we will climb onto the platform, the one on that train to the right. Why didn't I bring that damn scarf, we could have sold it, easy. Or given it as a present, everybody likes presents. Are you holding on?" We did not answer. We were holding on.

There was too much sun. I was squinting, and it seemed that mother was floating above ground. She was moving at a tremendous speed. But the soldier came. He said "You!" That was what he said to me. Then he pointed with his finger. Mother and Nina got to go on the train they had chosen from before, the one on the right, the one that went to a concentration camp. I got to go on the train to the left, the one that did not go to a concentration camp. This is not a confession.

Mother, Nina, and I were screaming, and crying, and all that other stuff. The train climbed quietly over the rails. It had a great rhythm. There was no air to breathe. There was no light to see. The only sense awake within me was hearing, and so I listened to that rhythm, I listened to it because I thought, "If this rhythm stops, I will die."

Four people jumped from that train. There was one survivor. Guess who it turned out to be? This is not a confession.

At night I hid out by the rails. An open- roofed train full of cattle and hay pulled up near dawn. I climbed into the cart full of hay, and buried myself in the damp sharp grasses. The train pulled out an hour later. That same rhythm began. The train wasn't any different, you know. Same rhythm, same cattle, and who would know the difference? For two days straight we rode without stop. I felt awake while sleeping, and asleep during the waking hours. The hay tasted like crap.

Chapter 1

We got to a city on the morning of the third day. I climbed out and found myself amidst a great market. I was lost to the world, lost to myself, and I was free. Not only was I free, but I was surrounded by food. I had no money, yet, it would be easy to steal. From the corner of my eye, I caught sight of a lovely fruit stand. As I walked toward it, I heard screams and shouts. I saw two men wrestling on the ground right next to it. One of them was trying to free a gun from his belt, and the other one lay beneath his feet, badly beaten.

I glanced at the beaten man and saw he had no weapon. Right next to me, on my right, there lay a carving board with a large knife prepared for customers tasting fruit. With one single reflex I pulled that knife and flung it at the man with the gun. He was already holding the gun in his hand at the moment when the knife pierced his chest. I took one look around the market and ran. There were many witnesses. A few men followed me, but soon got lost in the crowd.

The entire day was spent in dark corners and dirty neighborhoods. I was afraid of being identified. It was thrilling, in a way, that toss of the knife. Hundreds of times the boys and I played this game, stealing knives from the kitchen, making marks on trees, and then aiming from a distance. I was always one of the best. But that man, the way his blood squirted… Dark red, and thick. The way the blade reflected the sun light. I thought of mother. I thought of how she told us to be careful when we play with sharp things. I thought of how jealous Nina would get when I did not let her join our game of darts. "You're a girl! A little girl." And she was, but this is not a confession.

That evening, as I approached the train station in the dark, I heard the train slowly waking up from her day of rest. The puffing and coughing were now a comfort. I climbed back into the cart I had left, and buried myself once more in the hay. It was now warm and dry from standing in the sun all day. I wished for it to be like this forever.

Yet, in a few seconds I heard a rustling of hay coming from the other side of the cart. I tried not to breathe. The rhythm of the train was becoming steadier with every second. Soon the train was moving full speed. I must have fainted from fear because when I awoke it was morning and a man sat next to me.

Over my body like a blanket lay a soiled shirt, and next to me sat the man who was beaten up near the fruit stand. As I later found out, he was a thief. He was a great thief, with connections, and power over a large band of thieves. The man whom I killed was his second in command, and wanted to replace him as a leader. After I ran away and the curiosity of strangers subsided, he slipped away as well. He hid himself in the hay and when he heard me come tried not to make a sound. Finally, getting enough nerve, he uncovered me sleeping in the hay. Soon recognizing that it was I who saved his life, he took off his shirt and vowed to repay me in all the ways possible. He was in his late forties. His name was Maxim.

When we pulled into his city, a car was waiting for us. Men, bowing to him with all possible display of respect, treated us both as kings. He lived in eternal splendor and took me as his closest confidant. He called me his son, and all his men were kind and generous with me. I had the greatest teachers, books and games. Provided with everything I could ever need, and more, I grew up within this world of crime and gold into my teenage years.

One day Maxim called me into his bedroom. He looked tired and sick. His hair was thin and his face was wrinkled. These last ten years were hard for him. I knew he had been up for days. There was an unspoken sorrow among all the men. He said, "Everything will change Alex. I do not have much time. Everything always changes. You saved my life that day, and I have done my best to provide for you. You are the one good deed I have accomplished in this world. I have never involved you in any of my" he paused "my business transactions. I do not have time any more." Staring

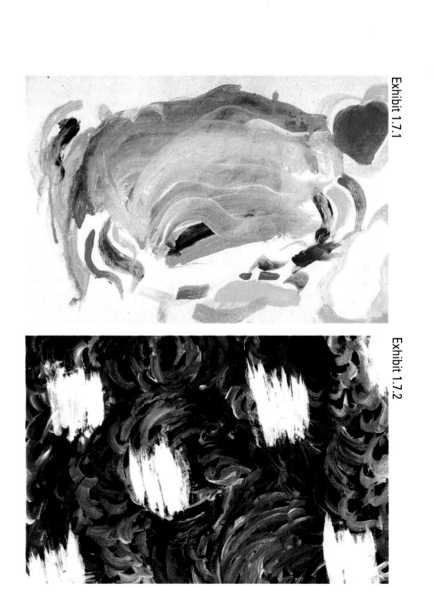

Exhibit 1.7.1

Exhibit 1.7.2

Chapter 1

right into my eyes, he asked, "What do you want to be, when you are older?" I thought for a minute. "I want to take pictures." I had always wanted to be a photographer. I wanted to remember things. I wanted to make others remember. To Maxim I said, "Thank you..."

The next day I had a suitcase in my room. Inside lay the latest, most modern camera known to man. Maxim wrote me a note saying that the camera was bought with absolutely clean money. Money he had once worked hard to earn. A ticket to another city lay there as well. I took the train out that very night. Three days later, I read that Maxim was found dead in his mansion.

I got a job at a photo studio in a small town. The work I did was great. I knew how to see things, how I wanted to see things. I walked around the city taking pictures of the people and places. The owner of the studio wanted my camera. The only logical way to deal with the problem seemed to be to eliminate me. I was accused of being a spy for the USA and Germany, and Japan.

It was '54 when they let me out. I had no family or friends. I did not know where I belonged, where my home was. I found a photo journalistic position in another small town. I even married a wife and had a daughter, but I never found true happiness in any of these actions. I entered an anonymous photography contest with an old photograph and was pleasantly surprised. The international finals were held in Paris and I had always dreamed of going there. My heart felt happiness once again. When I got to Paris and into my hotel room, memories of youth came back. I walked the streets and thought about many things. I read about a convention for survivors of the Holocaust held in Paris at the same time as the contest. I thought there might be a distant relative, or someone who knew my family, so I stopped by the office and submitted my last name.

I had forgotten about the entire incident when the phone of my hotel room rang. A friendly voice informed me that my mother and sister had been located living in France. They had moved to France when the camps were liberated. I stood in shock. My family... All these years... I did not know how to feel anymore. I was given two phone numbers. One was that of my sister, the other of my mother, who resided in a sanitarium.

I could not sleep, or eat, or think. I called the apartment of my sister first. I wanted to hear her pick up the phone. I wanted to hear her breathe on the other line. I wanted to say, "Nina, is that you?" and I knew she would recognize me. When I gathered my thoughts - as much as they could ever be gathered, - I picked up the phone and dialed. She picked up the phone, and said, "Hello, can I help you?" Her voice was a softness I had missed for years.

We spoke for hours, barely taking the time to breathe. She was so wonderful, and so vibrant. We decided that the very next day she would drive up to prepare mama for the reunion. She told me how mother always blamed herself for leaving me behind. She told me she would call me tomorrow and pick me up. That was the last time we spoke.

 I waited all day tomorrow and the day after that. Finally, two days later a man identifying himself as Nina's boss called my hotel room. I inquired about Nina and the quiet voice on the other line asked me whether I had not heard the terrible news. The man asked whether I was not aware that Nina perished in an automobile accident, yesterday evening, while on the way to visit her mother. "Not that this isn't horrible enough, but the old lady had a heart attack when she found out... Can you imagine?" He explained that Nina called him and told him the wonderful news. He said he knew about her death for a day now, but could not locate me until this moment. He said, "I am so very sorry about your loss..."

This is my life story. I went to the funeral. I brought pretty flowers and saw my family die for the second and the last time. I could not sleep. I have not slept in years - not really slept, anyway. I have this picture, where I stand and look over the two fresh graveyards. The day of death is the

Exhibit 1.7.3

Exhibit 1.7.4

Chapter 1

same on the two tombstones. This is my life story, and it is not a confession...

II

When Alex came into therapy, he did not fully understand his problems. He suffered from a lack of sleep and problems dealing with the other people in his life. The family claimed he was just a provider, and that he lacked the love and friendship necessary to good relationships.

Alex had never told the story of his life before. Not even his wife knew about his twisted past. In his early pictures, Alex begins to understand that his life is uncontrollable, full of pain, anger and blood (exhibit 1.7.1). He tries to portray his struggle towards an inner peace, a kind of redemption. As he spoke about his twisted fate, he paused to reflect on the doodles he had been drawing along with his story. "This is just like my twisted fate," he remarked with a sad grin.

In his next picture, much of his depression becomes apparent (exhibit 1.7.2) He is slowly understanding his sadness. The years of trying to be too many different people catch up to him. He realizes that never was a real thief, or a real photographer.

While searching for an escape from his routine and lonely life, Alex began drawing bright tangled lines (exhibit 1.7.3). "These are like the train tracks," he said. "They are all tangled. I was forced to go down some of them by life's circumstance. Some of them I chose because it was easier to be numb."

At the end of therapy, Alex did understand that his troubles stemmed from more than just loneliness. The rose stands alone (exhibit 1.7.1). Present are the two forces in Alex's life: darkness and light. There are black moons, and yet he looks out towards the sun.

Alex wanted to take another chance with people. He wanted to tell his story until the truth was heard, but unfortunately he died of a serious heart condition shortly after the therapy was complete. He was coming to terms with his own boundaries, his own choices, and his own confessions. This, however, is not one of them.

Chapter 1

Clinical information

ALEX
Sixty six years old white male.
Skinny, disshaved, unkempt dressed, looking angry

Axis   I: Major Depressive Disorder,- 296.33
Axis II: None
Axis III: None
Axis IV: Stressor –isolation, life tragedy.
Axis V: GAF at the beginning of treatment = 30.GAF at discharge = 79

Treatment approaches:
Art therapy;
Psychoanalysis;
Cognitive – behavioral approach.

Duration of treatment:
Thirty eight sessions.

Chapter II

People Draw Their Mood

Chapter 2

This chapter explores some of the differences among the paintings produced by people with one of four disorders: adjustment disorder, anxiety disorder, depression, or post-traumatic stress disorder. It attempts to identify features that are characteristic of each disorder, but that does not imply that the presence of these elements in a painting means that the artist needs therapy! Rather it can mean that the artist experienced feelings similar to those experienced by people with the disorder (such as sadness, or nervousness, or confusion) at the time of making a painting. In fact it is possible to illustrate each disorder using examples from world art. Many elements characteristic of adjustment disorder (as well as overall mood) are present in paintings by Hopper. Paintings by both Van Gogh and Bosch could illustrate art works produced by people with anxiety disorders. Paintings by O'Keeffe are in many ways similar to those painted by people with depression. And the early art of Kandinsky as well as that of De Kooning are much like art produced by people with post-traumatic stress disorder.

In general, some themes are more common then others – for example, about a third of all paintings are abstract. However, each disorder has its own set of "favorite" themes. Similarly, the paints given to all patients were the same – a standard set of red, yellow, green, blue, white, and so on. But the colors most often chosen are different for each disorder. By use of different sets of colors, strokes, and compositions, these people were able to express their emotions, the nature and intensity of which varied from disorder to disorder. Here is a brief look at those differences.

Drawings by people with adjustment disorder often contain a single object or a few objects, one of which is set apart or is different from the rest. In many other drawings some kind of division is present. Composition is usually centered and fairly simple. In "overall" pictures the center is indicated. There seem to be no special preferences for colors; conventional color combinations are used. People with adjustment disorder prefer to draw people. Other popular themes include animals and words.

Drawings by people with anxiety disorder tend to be very crowded. Either they include many objects or they are painted using many short and active strokes. There are often many diagonals and active curves. The organization is busy, with no composition. Concrete subjects are not popular at all with people in this group, least popular themes being animals and words. The colors are often bright, and contrasts are sharp but not unconventional.

Drawings by people with depression tend to be arranged around a vertical or horizontal axis. They are often minimal and calm. In some the stroke is very smooth, while in others it is flowing, not active. The colors are often muted or watered down and pale, the contrasts are mild. Blues and grays are used a lot, and black is common. There are many monochromes. The themes of the drawings are often inanimate and emotionally neutral - flowers, nature, landscapes, buildings.

Drawings by people with post-traumatic stress disorder tend to be very unsettling. The objects are not necessarily appropriate for the subject matter, yet they are vaguely concrete. The color combinations are very unconventional and sharp. The colors are often do not correspond to the realistic colors of the object depicted. The composition is usually very simple and organized. Interestingly enough, people with post-traumatic stress disorder did not have any special preferences for any topics, and the distribution of themes in this category reflected general distribution across groups.

These brief descriptions, however, are far from complete. The next segment explores finer distinctions in imagery, and attempts to connect these differences to the mental state of the artist.

Chapter 2

Adjustment

Paintings by people with adjustment disorders tend to concentrate on establishing identity and making sense of the external world. The confusion created by the disorder is dealt with by defining each object as clearly as possible. This is achieved in a variety of ways, some of which are obvious and some more subtle.

The problems are addressed in a very direct ways. The problem of identity is addressed by painting people (a most common theme of paintings in this group), and stating one's name either as a theme of the painting (see 2.1.14, 2.1.16, 2.1.19), or as a signature (see 2.1.1, 2.1.6, 2.1.11, 2.1.15). The problem of trying to make sense of the world is dealt with by depicting objects in very stereotypical manner, the way they "should be"(see 2.1.2, 2.1.3, 2.1.7, 2.1.8, 2.1.9, 2.1.18). Some paintings contain further clarifications: the portrayed object is identified in writing (see 2.1.6, 2.1.20) and the feeling is depicted just with the use of words and common symbols (see 2.1.13, 2.1.15). Abstract paintings, although numerous, are less popular.

The issue of clarity is pursued not only in the choice of imagery, but also in construction of composition and in choice of colors. The composition is usually centered (see 2.1.2, 2.1.7, 2.1.9, 2.1.10, 2.1.12, 2.1.13, 2.1.14, 2.1.16, 2.1.18, 2.1.20), and very conventional: the entire surface of canvas is used, and conventional elements surround the main subject of the painting. The colors used are usually primary and very clear (see 2.1.10, 2.1.13, 2.1.14, 2.1.17, 2.1.19, 2.1.20). Mixed colors are unusual. Contours are usually neatly defined, and the shapes are clearly divided from each other (see 2.1.2, 2.1.10, 2.1.17, 2.1.18).

Besides being clear in general, these paintings tend to be fairly clear on the individual level as well. Since people with this disorder have a pretty clear idea of what bothers them (or at least think that they do), clear references to their feelings appear in their paintings. Some reflect nostalgia for the lost environment (see 2.1.3, 2.1.7, 2.1.20), again depicted in a very stereotypical manner. Others depict an imaginary and idealistic world (see 2.1.2, 2.1.10, 2.1.12) as an escape from the discomforts of this world. Sometimes the patient feels unable to fit in as a result of feelings of inadequacy. This too finds its way into the paintings, taking a rather rudimentary form: he depicts himself among others of the same kind or within an environment, but as qualitatively different and unfit (see 2.1.5, 2.1.10). Other paintings depict the artist as being different from his or her surrounding, but in a favorable way. The idea is that "not only am I different, I am also better." These paintings often depict the artist as an imaginary character, such as a princess (see 2.1.4, 2.1.9, 2.1.12).

In general, almost all of the paintings depict an object at rest; the portrayal of movement is a rare occurrence. This is consistent with an overall preoccupation with clarity characteristic of this group. The depictions take the form of catalog items, shown as unobstructed as possible.

Exhibit 2.1.1

Exhibit 21.3

Exhibit 2.1.4

Exhibit 2.1.5

Exhibit 2.1.6

Exhibit 2.1.7

Exhibit 2.1.8

Exhibit 2.1.13

Exhibit 2.1.14

Exhibit 2.1.15

Exhibit 2.1.16

Exhibit 2.1.17

Exhibit 2.1.2

Exhibit 2.1.9

Exhibit 2.1.10

Exhibit 2.1.11

Exhibit 2.1.12

Exhibit 2.1.18

Exhibit 2.1.19

Exhibit 2.1.20

Chapter 2

Anxiety Disorder

Paintings created by people with anxiety disorder are almost exactly opposite to the ones created by people with adjustment disorder. The source of their discomfort is not concrete and not obvious to them. This confusion results in much less concrete and much more complex paintings. The popular themes among this category are abstract paintings, paintings of city life and of still life/collages. These topics lend themselves well to the expressions of uncertainty and fear characteristic of this disorder.

Almost all of the paintings in this category portray movement (see 2.2.1,2.2.5, 2.2.6, 2.2.7, 2.2.8, 2.2.9, 2.2.17, 2.2.19). Even abstract paintings and stationary objects appear to be moving. This is achieved through placing many objects on the canvas (see 2, 3, 9, 11, 13, 15) and using very active lines (such as wiggling lines (see 2.2.1, 2.2.7, 2.2.8, 2.2.9, 2.2.15, 2.2.19) and diagonals (see 2.2.5, 2.2.6, 2.2.14, 2.2.17). Such a high level of activity communicates a high level of nervousness and restlessness, characteristic of the disorder.

Most paintings are very crowded. Not only are there many objects or forms, but in many instances the same form is repeated many times (see 2.2.1, 2.2.2, 2.2.4, 2.2.5, 2.2.9, 2.2.13, 2.2.15, 2.2.19). It seems that for this people it is very important to release their inner tension through hectic monotonous actions, resulting in multiples of the same shape packed close on the surface of the canvas. These forms do not contribute anything to the overall meaning of the painting; they just make it look more busy. Since abstract paintings lend themselves well to this type of patterning, they are very popular in that group.

Although in many cases people with this disorder do not know the exact reason for their distress, some paintings show threatening themes as reflection of the artist's anxiety (see 2.2.7, 2.2.10, 2.2.17). These direct portrayals of stress evoking situations are rare, however. In most cases the feeling of fear is portrayed in less direct ways. One such "symbol of distress" is the color red, which is present in almost all paintings (see 2.2.1, 2.2.2, 2.2.3, 2.2.5, 2.2.6, 2.2.7, 2.2.9, 2.2.11,2.2.12, 2.2.14, 2.2.15, 2.2.17, 2.2.18, 2.2.19). The feeling of vulnerability is portrayed through showing colors as mixing and infiltrating each other (see 2.2.3, 2.2.4, 2.2.5, 2.2.6, 2.2.12, 2.2.14, 2.2.16).

The compositions are usually not structured. Objects often fill space without any order governing their placement (see 2.2.2,2.2.3,2.2.9,2.2.11,2.2.14), and they often are not tied together very well (see 2.2.7, 2.2.10, 2.2.18, 2.2.19). Other paintings seem to be very strictly organized, as if the artist was trying to suppress his or her anxiety (see 2.2.4, 2.2.13, 2.2.15).

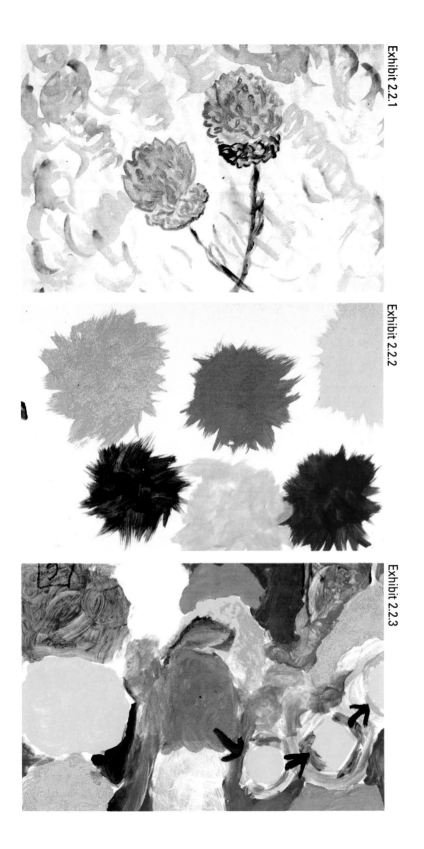

Exhibit 2.2.1

Exhibit 2.2.2

Exhibit 2.2.3

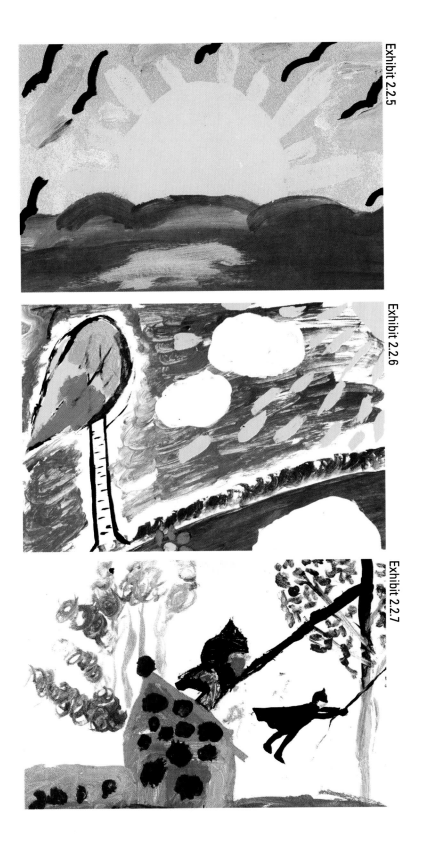

Exhibit 2.2.5

Exhibit 2.2.6

Exhibit 2.2.7

Exhibit 2.2.4

Exhibit 2.2.8

Exhibit 2.2.10

Exhibit 2.2.9

Exhibit 2.2.11

Exhibit 2.2.12

Exhibit 2.2.13

Exhibit 2.2.14

Exhibit 2.2.15

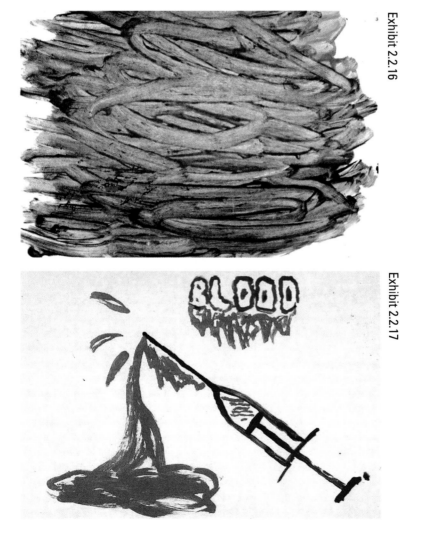

Exhibit 2.2.16

Exhibit 2.2.17

Exhibit 2.2.18

Exhibit 2.2.19

Chapter 2

Depression

The overall feeling that is communicated by paintings done by people with depression is that of stagnation. They often deal with detached but concrete subjects, such as nature and still life, which contain low emotional content. Portraits of people and animals as well as other active and/or emotional topics are avoided. Flat affect and lack of energy, common among people with depression, are strongly evident in the paintings in this category.

In most cases objects portrayed by depressed people (in contrast to those portrayed by people with anxiety disorder) are stationary. They are either portrayals of objects that in general don't move (such as buildings 2.3.17 and cosmic bodies 2.3. 4) or portrayals of inanimate objects as stationary, against a blank background (see 2.3.1, 2.3.3, 2.3.8, 2.3.18, 2.3.19), reminiscent of illustrations in a catalog. If an object is depicted within a natural environment, it is still stagnant: scenes of nature captured at the windless, quiet moment (see 2.3.6, 2.3.7). When there is movement in the picture, it is very regular, calm and wavy (see 2.3.5, 2.3.9, 2.3.11, 2.3.12). This regularity and repetition of pattern actually create a further sense of stability.

Depictions of more emotionally involving themes, such as depictions of people, animals and words, also follow the general pattern of detachment and stagnation. The figures are either completely stable (and look like as if can remain in their assumed positions for another year (see 2.3.10, 2.3.20), that in part making them appear sad, or, if they are moving, then the move-ment is again regular and wavy, and the figures themselves tend to be abstracted and unrealistic (see 2.3.9, 2.3.11). In general, among people with depression, the paintings that depict inanimate objects tend to be realistic, and the ones that deal with people and animals tend to be abstracted, reflecting an evident tactic in dealing with more unsettling themes.

Further sense of stability is achieved in most of these paintings by organizing composition along the vertical axis (see 2.3.1, 2.3.3, 2.3.7, 2.3.18, 2.3.19) or horizontal (see 2.3.4, 2.3.5, 2.3.8, 2.3.15). This simple organization effectively serves to anchor the image and to minimize movement. Diagonals are much less common, since they represent a more active organization. The simplicity of organization is further reinforced by simplicity of composition. Often a single object is depicted, and the background is either very simple and minimal (see 2.3.2, 2.3.6, 2.3.7, 2.3.13, 2.3.15) or is entirely omitted (see 2.3.1, 2.3.3, 2.3.8, 2.3.14, 2.3.18, 2.3.19). This minimalist approach deepens the sense of apathy; it is as though the artist lacked the strength or interest to elaborate on the theme. Some pictures are even left unfinished (see 2.3.6.) and others are done in pencil, more like sketches then paintings (see 2.3.8, 2.3.14, 2.3.18).

The colors used by people with depression are usually muted (see 2.3.1, 2.3.4, 2.3.11, 2.3.13, 2.3.16) or watered down (see 2.3.2, 2.3.5, 2.3.8, 2.3.12,2.3.14). Bright colors are rare; even red is either muted (see 2.3.1) or watered and softened (see 2.3.13). There are a lot of grays and different shades of blue (reflecting the metaphor of "feeling blue"). Sharp contrasts are also uncommon. Usually the entire painting is done in colors of the same intensity (see 2.3.1, 2.3.2, 2.3.5, 2.3.11, 2.3.12). This is the only category where monochromes are very common (see 2.3.4, 2.3.8, 2.3.14, 2.3.15, 2.3.16, 2.3.17, 2.3.18, 2.3.19) - again, a clear indication of apathy.

Exhibit 2.3.1

Exhibit 2.3.2

Exhibit 2.3.5

Exhibit 2.3.3

Exhibit 2.3.4

Exhibit 2.3.6

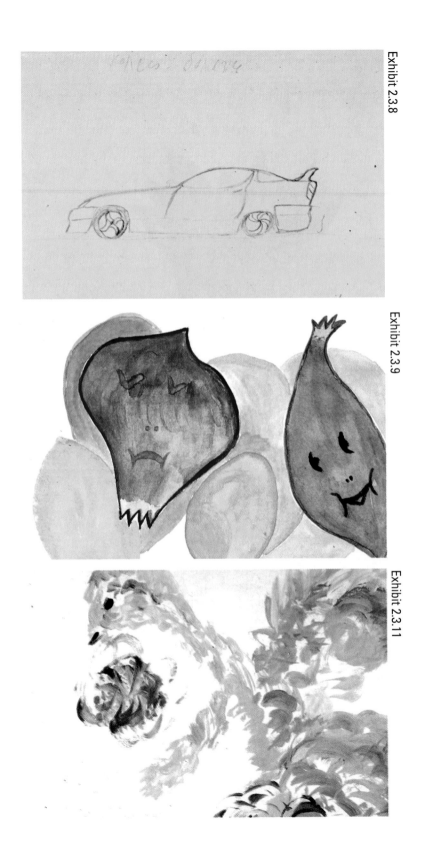

Exhibit 2.3.8

Exhibit 2.3.9

Exhibit 2.3.11

Exhibit 2.3.7

Exhibit 2.3.10

Exhibit 2.3.12

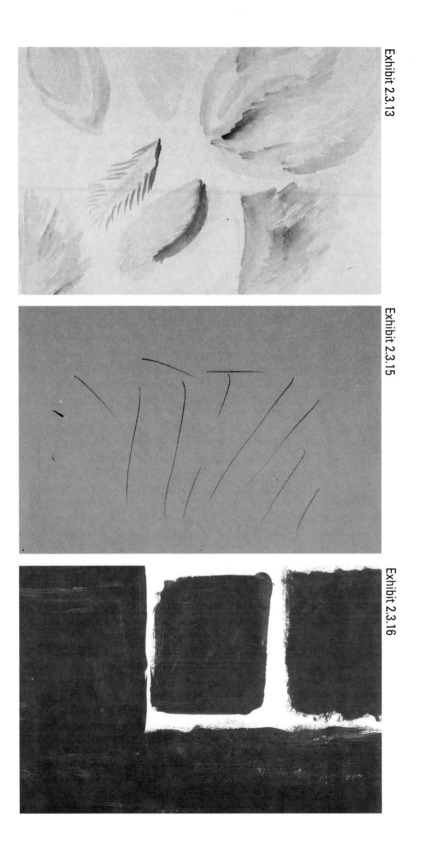

Exhibit 2.3.13

Exhibit 2.3.15

Exhibit 2.3.16

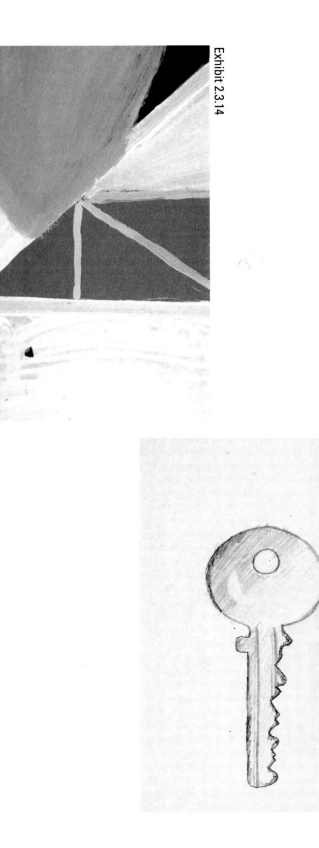

Exhibit 2.3.14

Exhibit 2.3.19

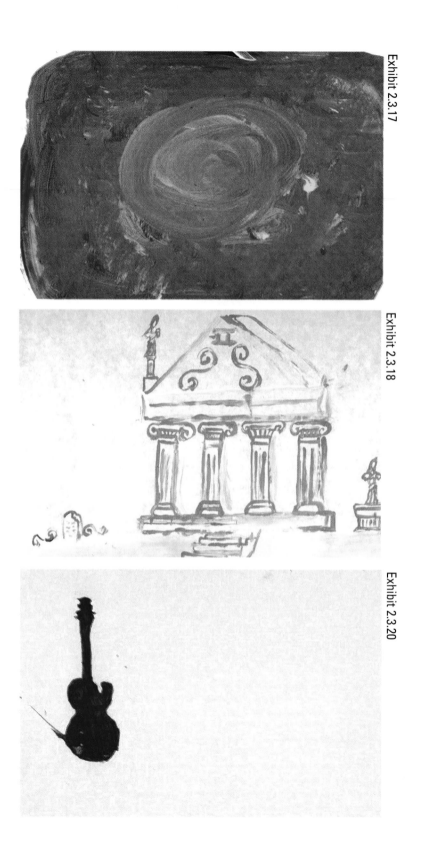

Exhibit 2.3.17

Exhibit 2.3.18

Exhibit 2.3.20

Chapter 2

Post-Traumatic Stress Disorder

The paintings in this category are characterized by an overwhelming sense of horror and – though it may sound medieval – of doom. The danger is present and imminent, and while not entirely concrete, is yet not entirely abstract. There seems to be no preference for any particular theme, but all of the paintings are alike in the sense that they all seem to be violent and disturbing.

The feeling of being threatened is communicated through portraying objects on a painting as falling (see 2.4.1, 2.4.6, 2.4.8, 2.4.10), flying through the air (see 2.4.16, 2.4.17), exploding (see 2.4.9, 2.4.15), or threatening (see 2.4.11, 2.4.18,2.4.19). In other cases an oversized form dominates a painting. This form could be concrete and representing either an object or a part of an object (see 2.4.2, 2.4.3, 2.4.6, 2.4.7, 2.4.19), or abstract and unrecognizable (see 2.4.5, 2.4.8, 2.4.12, 2.4.13, 2.4.20). Whether concrete or abstract, this shape represents something overwhelming and overpowering that these people feel unable to overcome or cope with.

Appropriately enough, many of the paintings are similar to those painted by people with anxiety disorder. In both groups there is a lot of movement: both factual - walking (see 2.4.13), swinging (see 2.4.9, 2.4.11) and flying (see 2.4.12, 2.44.20) – and also deriving from the use of active strokes (see 2.4.1, 2.4.7, 2.4.15, 2.4.16, 2.4.17, 2.4.18) and composition (see 2.4.5, 2.4.8, 2.4.14, 2.4.17, 2.4.18, 2.4.19). The entire surface of the painting is usually utilized, with more than one object depicted; however, unlike the paintings produced by people with anxiety, these do not seem crowded.

What makes these paintings particularly violent is frequent presence of bright red splashes   of color, often similar in form to the splashes of blood (see 2.4.1.1,2.4.4,2.4.9,2.4.14,2.4.15,2.4.16,2.4.17,2.4.18,2.4.19). Depictions of thorns (see 2.4.1, 2.4.4,2.4.15) and knives (see 2.4.11,2.4.19), as well as an abundance of sharp angles (see 2.4.2, 2. 4.3, 2.4.5,2.4.14) only add to this feeling.

When looking at many of the paintings in this group, the feeling that arises is that something is not right. Some, as I mentioned earlier, depict clearly violent themes (see 2.4.11, 2.4.18, 2.4.19), and even the ones that do not outwardly concentrate on violence still include references to cutting, blood, etc. However, there is more to it. The colors that are put into immediate contact with each other are usually unconventionally matched, such as bright primary colors with black (see 2.4.14,2.4.16,2.4.18). Red is present on almost all of the paintings, and usually in its primary form. Some elements seem inappropriate, such as outlining of the sunrays (see 2.4.5) and light pink shape (see 2.4.20) in black. Lack of feet on all depictions of the people (see 2.4.9,2.4.10,2.4.18, 2.4.19), and the presence of an abstract form in a painting that otherwise deals with a realistic matter also seem unusual.

People in this category in general seem to pay little attention to details; many paintings seem to have been painted hastily, in quick strokes, with no emphasis on accuracy or decorative elements. Some forms are only semi-recognizable (see 2.4.3, 2.4.4, 2.4.6, 2.4.9, 2.4.10). One phrase to describe all of them would be "on the run." Apparently the topics depicted are too traumatic to deal with extensively.

Exhibit 2.4.1

Exhibit 2.4.6

Exhibit 2.4.2

Exhibit 2.4.3

Exhibit 2.4.4

Exhibit 2.4.5

Exhibit 2.4.7

Exhibit 2.4.9

Exhibit 2.4.10

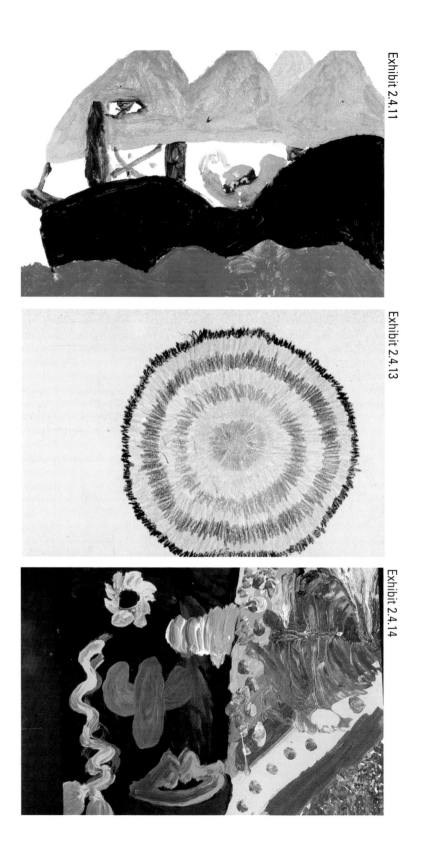

Exhibit 2.4.11

Exhibit 2.4.13

Exhibit 2.4.14

Exhibit 2.4.15

Exhibit 2.4.16

Exhibit 2.4.17

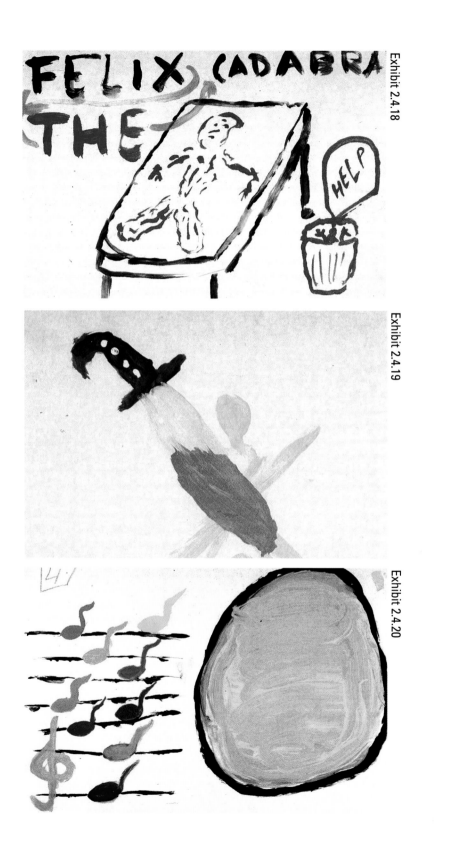

Exhibit 2.4.18

Exhibit 2.4.19

Exhibit 2.4.20

Exhibit 2.4.8

Exhibit 2.4.12

Chapter III

Adolescent Groups Drawing and Talking

Chapter 3

For the past eight years I have led adolescent art therapy groups. The process of art therapy can be altered to fit the unique needs of group work. The topics of the discussions vary, depending on the needs and interests of a particular group. Often, it is the adolescents themselves who bring up the topic that is important to them. In this type of setting, the drawing process parallels the discussion, occurring at the same time. While the group is involved in the conversation, each individual member is presented with the palette, paper, and a brush, and is asked to draw during the discussion.

Chapter 3

Use of palettes

At the end of the session, everyone is asked to take his or her palette (a paper plate with different paints that were used for the drawings), and to mix the paint on the palette any way they choose. After observing many individuals mix their palettes, I have noticed a particular pattern, that would emerge for every individual. Each palette tends to reflect the individual's feelings and emotions that were experienced during the session. Not only were the discussion themes apparent on the palettes, but so were the individual's unique experiences and feelings. Interestingly enough, examination of an individual's drawings during the group session together with his or her palette points to the relationship between them.

Teenagers are often intimidated and embarrassed when asked to draw a picture. Frequently, they say that they "simply cannot draw", and are "not good artists". Palettes thus allow for a less intimidating experience with the paint. Mixing a palette is not viewed as creating a drawing; rather, it is a fun, somewhat cathartic experience. Due to the nature of the task, as well as the time when it is performed (the end of the session), palettes reflect a whole array of feelings and emotions that were evoked and experienced during the session. This non-threatening exercise allows an attentive observer a glimpse into thee unconscious.

This chapter presents drawings and palettes from two adolescent groups. Each group consisted of from fifteen and a half to sixteen and half-year-old adolescents with different cultural and socio-economic backgrounds. The adolescents who were familiar with the process did the drawings shown. They have had a few experiences with palettes, and knew how the colors tend to mix. Hence, although the result of the mixing reflects many unconscious feelings and emotions, the process of mixing is somewhat conscious, and the point when these individuals choose to stop mixing is a conscious decision.

Let us proceed with the examination of the drawings, and discuss how individuals' palettes parallel their drawings.

Chapter 3

Adolescent Group 1.

At the beginning of the session, a group member brought up a personal experience that was disturbing and upsetting to him. The same day at school, this teenager had been asked to write an essay about something in his life that he was feeling ashamed of. This boy had written a story about killing a cat. Later, he decided to share this experience with the group. The synopsis of the story is as follows:

When this boy was little, a homeless cat lived on his street. This cat bothered him a great deal, and he decided to kill it. He tied the cat to a tree, poured some gasoline on it, and set it on fire. He then watched the cat scream, trying to escape, and finally die.

This story provoked a lengthy discussion among the group members. The topics varied, with each adolescent commenting on the emotions that the story produced. More general subjects of love, patience, indifference, anger, were brought up during the discussion. Later, the discussion shifted to the topic of abuse. The group talked about how people should be treated, and how to deal with one's anger. At the end of the session, many group members felt angry and frustrated. Painful experiences of being hurt, offended, and mistreated, had surfaced by the end of the session. The four drawings and palettes are presented here to demonstrate how the use of color, pictorial content, and the choice of particular objects indicate an individual's feelings and emotions at the time of the drawing.

Consider how the use of red color reflects emotions of hurt and violence on the 3.1.1A and the palette 3.1.1B. Within the red frame on a palette, this girl had drawn her face. Contours are not neatly defined on this palette; the face is just floating in the middle without shape or connection. Similarly, the heart on the drawing 3.1.1A is also floating on the background of washed-away, pastel colors. The heart is enclosed within the black frame. It appears to be bleeding inside. The striking contrast between colors used for the heart and the colors used for the background parallels the group's discussion of feeling hurt and alone in the cold, unsafe world.

Drawing 3.1.2A and its correspondent palette 3.1.2B utilize a variety of bright colors to portray the explosion of fire. As in many drawings of people who are experiencing anxiety, there is a sense of movement in both the picture and the palette. In the picture, the more concrete image of a face, with mouth wide open, is placed aside from the fire that is burning everything around. On a more abstract level, the palette speaks of the same feelings of anxiety and hurt by using an explosion of bright colors. While the first person was able to contain most of the feelings within a frame of a heart, this individual is having more difficulty handling all the emotions. The drawing and the palette portray this emotional explosion.

The face on the drawing 3.1.3A is distorted with anger. Enlarged ears and wide mouth speak of this individual's world of sensory stimuli. This person can speak and hear, yet everything is seen though the red lens of anger. Notice that like the two drawings above, this one too is floating in the air, having no connection with the world. As on its corresponding palette, 3.1.3B, the colors are mixed together with no specific pattern, except a couple of splashes of bright red and blue. A sense of lost identity and confusion, as well as the feelings of frustration and anger, is communicated through the use of abstract shapes and the choice of colors.

Drawing 3.1.4A is more concrete, portraying a fire burning in the otherwise peaceful surroundings. This peace is about to be destroyed by the fire that is growing bigger. The dark

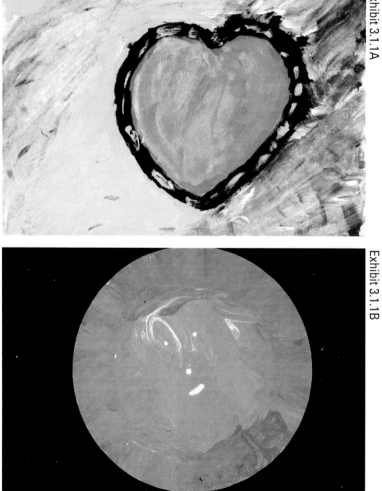

Exhibit 3.1.1A

Exhibit 3.1.1B

Exhibit 3.1.2A

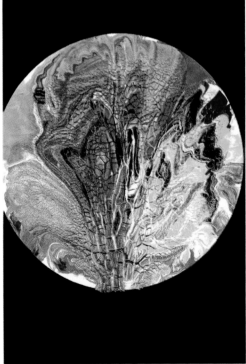

Exhibit 3.1.2B

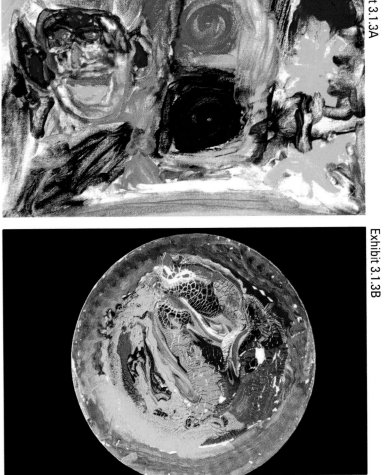

Exhibit 3.1.3A

Exhibit 3.1.3B

Exhibit 3.1.4A

Exhibit 3.1.4B

Chapter 3

emotions are ʀɛflected in this youth's palette, which is mixed so that the col᷄   ᷄e
messy dark composition, with sharp, threatening edges around them.

Examination of the drawings produced by this group allows to see the recurring pattern: the more concrete theme (the burning of the cat) in most of the drawings corresponds to more abstract expression on the palettes of the emotions the story evoked.

Adolescent Group 2.

This group discussed parent-child relationship. Developmentally, the need for autonomy and self-expression conflicts with the concern about separation from the parents. Drawing 3.2.1A shows how this adolescent feels. He is locked inside the protective walls of the castle, built by his parents. In fact, both of them are standing by the doors, guarding his world, and letting in only those whom they consider trustworthy. The few small windows do not allow this boy to see the whole picture of the world. The walls of the castle are smooth and tall, while the pointed roofs add to its war-like appearance. Being trapped inside this house with every possible exit guarded, produces anxiety. Perhaps before it felt like a safe heaven, but now, when the adolescent is ready to experience the world on his owns, he feels trapped. The palette (3.2.B) shows similar feelings; the colors are all blended together, and the palette looks like a globe. Yet, there are no distinct shapes or forms: the world is confusing and distant as if seen from the small windows of a castle. Similarly, the theme of drawing 3.2.2A reflects the anxiety of another adolescent. The drawing is made of distinct lines that have clear borders between them. Bright colors are followed by darker, deeper colors. She views her life as a distinct pattern of events and emotions that do not blend together: anxiety, hope, and depression follow each other but do not mix. The palette 3.2.2B further uncovers the story, showing that even though some events in this youth's life are happy, on a deeper level she feels depressed and sad, with more sadness right at the center of her being.

Many adolescents crave freedom from parental guidance, yet at the same time feel confused and scared by the necessity for making independent decisions. The drawing 3.2.4A presents a portrayal of this youth's world. The huge world that she soon will encounter on her own is rather frightening. On one hand, breaking it into smaller pieces makes it less threatening, more approachable. On the other hand, having to deal with the myriad of various issues creates anxiety and confusion for this girl. The palette (3.2.4B) shows the whole array of mixed feelings that this adolescent is currently experiencing.

Youths of this age are also in the process of creating a self-identity that is somewhat different from that of their parents. The need to define and integrate one's personal beliefs with the general rules of behavior that were inflicted on the adolescent by his or her parents and society is often a cause for anxiety. The drawing 3.2.3A reflects these feelings. Having recently left Russia, this youth is feeling confused about his religious and cultural identities. In Russia, this boy was perceived and treated as a Jew. Now, many Americans refer him to as a 'Russian'. Suddenly, he is seen as a representative of a country that his parents chose to leave, and of a culture that often treated him as a foreigner. While this teenager is struggling to establish a sense of personal identity, changes in his environment prolong the state of confusion. His parents are also giving him mixed messages. They expect him to retain his Russian language and to participate in a cultural life of immigrant society. At the same time, they would like him to learn and understand an American culture, hoping that he will accept this country as his new

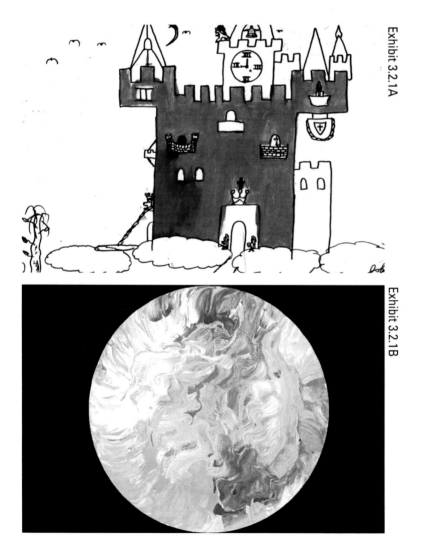

Exhibit 3.2.1A

Exhibit 3.2.1B

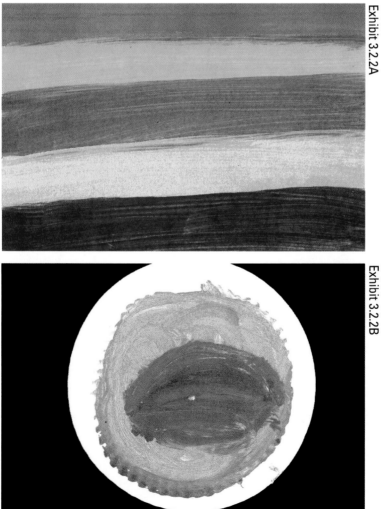

Exhibit 3.2.2A

Exhibit 3.2.2B

Exhibit 3.2.3A

Exhibit 3.2.3B

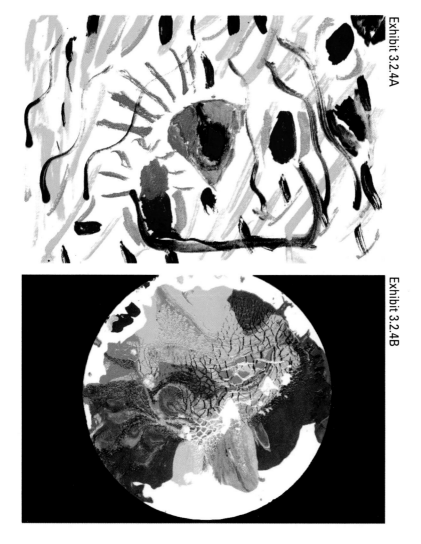

Exhibit 3.2.4A

Exhibit 3.2.4B

Chapter 3

homeland. Integrating these somewhat conflicting concepts to form a sense of cultural and personal identity presents a serious challenge to many immigrant teenagers. Notice the cross on
the picture that reminds of a tombstone standing on a grave where the past is buried. One solu-
tion of the identity dilemma is to forget one's past and to begin building a completely different
life in a completely new country. The palette 3.2.3B symbolizes the feelings of confusion and
sadness that this teenager is experiencing by blending all the dark colors together.

        Establishing a trusting rapport with a helper and feeling safe sharing their anxieties is
often a very difficult and even threatening experience for many teenagers. Group art therapy
provides a non-threatening environment, where sharing of 'cohort' problems can occur through
the discussion, while very personal experiences can be expressed and shared through the use of
drawings. The drawings and the palettes of the adolescents in this group reflect many concerns
that are unique to that age group and individual personality.

CHAPTER IV

Adoptive Children Draw Their Life

Chapter 4

For the past four years, I have been working with American families who were going through the process of adopting a child or children from different countries. After working with these children, I began seeing how different and unique were their needs in comparison to the same age peers. In addition to being behind in passing regular developmental milestones, such as starting to talk, walk, and being toilet trained adopted children are facing issues that even many adults have difficulty handling. Processes of adapting to living in a new family environment parallel the processes of acculturation and assimilation to the new country, culture, and language. For many adopted children, the whole concept of 'family' is foreign. Because the majority come from foster homes, where they lacked warmth and loving that most of their peers receive from parents, these children experience separation anxiety and exhibit tremendous fear that their new parents will abandon them. The drawings of adapted children reflect a whole spectrum of such feelings and emotions.

To get a better sense for how children's pictures helped with the process of building a new adoptive family, I included the statement of the adoptive mother. This is a practical application of the theories described below.

My name is Judy Schwartz, and my husband Robert and I adopted four wonderful children, Lindsay, age 11, Emily, age 7, Matthew, age 8, and Logan, age 4. Lindsay was adopted at birth domestically, Emily, Matthew and Logan were adopted in August, 1996 from Tula, Russia.

Our experience of an international adoption was very positive. We traveled to Russia with our eldest daughter to meet and bring home her new siblings.

Once home, we faced many frustrations in trying to create a family out of a group of strangers. We had a language barrier as well as a cultural one. Our children had never lived in a "normal" family, although they were by birth, siblings. One method used to try to communicate desires and fears was having the children draw pictures for us. These drawings helped our children to communicate their needs and worries to us. As parents, we used these pictures to understand their feelings better. Through the changes of these drawings, we saw how well our children were adjusting to their new lives.

We noticed that in these drawings, the children would make very large houses, we assumed these houses represented the huge brick building where they lived in the orphanage in Tula. There were always big trees and grass around the houses, or brown representing the dirt that was there in lieu of the grass. They did not draw any figures, not even to represent the orphanage staff that cared for them. The children really expressed their anxieties through their artwork. Later on, when they developed enough language, they told us more about their feelings that we saw before mostly in their pictures.

As the children adjusted to their new lives, their artwork changed as well. Houses still were the main objects of their pictures, but they became smaller and sometimes there would only be a part instead of the whole house. They did not pay much attention to coloring the windows with yellow light (sometimes they even forgot to draw the windows at all). Later on, people were added into these pictures. Always there was a big lady who was Mommy, and a big man, who was Daddy. Occasionally there was a child or children, but for a long time, just the two caretaking adults. As the parental figures grew bigger, demonstrating greater importance and security to the children, the houses and trees grew smaller and less elaborate. The pictures of Mommy and Daddy became more full of detail, capturing Daddy's beard, or Mommy's curly red hair. They showed their increased attachment to us in their artwork.

Exhibit 4.1

Exhibit 4.2

Exhibit 4.3

Exhibit 4.4

Exhibit 4.5

Exhibit 4.6

Exhibit 4.7

Exhibit 4.8

Chapter 4

Our experience of adopting three Russian born children was amazing. We look back at that first year with such wonder as to how we survived the stress and at how terrific our children are and how well adjusted they are. Considering all the changes that they had to go through, they have done remarkably well in less than two years. They did not know how to kiss or hug, they did not know how to show or receive affection. It took countless attempts to show how to give a kiss, similar to how one teaches an infant to do so. We taught them boundaries, made them feel safe, showed them compassion, and gave them a lot of love and affection to bring them to where they are today. During the first three months there was absolutely no communication between us except a lot of gesturing. We had to discipline and teach them right from wrong without being able to speak to them in a language they could understand. We counted on facial expressions to help get our points across. We rarely relied on someone translating for us. That was used for emergencies such as telling the children not to go into the street, as they did not have any knowledge of cars and the dangers of traffic, or explaining that they were going to go to school and that we would pick them up after. We wanted them to learn to rely upon us, to trust us and know that when we said something it was important that they listen and do as we asked. This came about around the fourth and fifth month, when their changeover to English from Russian was occurring. It seemed that one night they went to sleep speaking and understanding Russian, and when they awoke, they were speaking and understanding English. Sadly, as they learned to think, speak and express themselves in English, they lost all knowledge of Russian. They could not recall their Russian names after two weeks of being called by their English names. This was remarkable to me, especially with Emily who had her Russian name for five years. She has limited memory of her life in Russia, although we have encouraged her to tell us about her experiences. She states, when asked, that her life here is so good that she does not like to think of life in Russia. Her love for us is based a lot on the fact that we are good to her. For Mother's day, she wrote me a story and made me pictures, depicting her life in our family. She stated that she loves her Mommy because her Mommy is so sweet to her. She is a soft and gentle child, a natural born caregiver. Matthew makes many pictures for us in kindergarten, and all are of his family. He is always the biggest person in the group, and all of us are surrounding him. His pictures used to be barren and empty, now they are filled with the love he knows he has in his life. Logan, who is still in pre-school, draws as any normal almost five-year-old. He has absolutely no memory of anything but life in our family. Matthew does not recall his life elsewhere, but his art has reflected differently. Emily has carried memories that are slowly being replaced with happiness and wonderful experiences. Our lives have been greatly enhanced by this experience and everyday when I look at my children, I see four healthy, happy, loved human beings that I know will make a positive difference in our world. I think of what their futures might have been like, what mine and my husband's lives would be like without them, and I truly feel the hand of God in this miracle I call my family."

The drawings of recently adapted youngsters tend to focus around the main issue of adapting to the new family environment. They express the most immediate concern: Do I belong in this family? Am I good enough for them? The curiosity that the children possess of why their new parents adopted them raises their level of anxiety. They start wondering what qualities should they have or develop in order to fit and be accepted by the new family and environment. These young children are faced with the necessity to deal with the identity issues that are far beyond their conceptual abilities.

Chapter 4

Many children have difficulty understanding that their new family will not send them back to foster home, even if they misbehave or do something wrong. This most irrational anxiety is often the central area of concern for most of the newly adopted children. Some of them deal with it by developing conduct problems and testing the limits of their parents' alleged love. Other youngsters decide that they need to stand up to their new parents' expectations by becoming exemplary children. They are afraid to do or say anything that might lead their new parents to decide to send them back. Unfortunately, this anxiety is persistent and irrational, and it takes a long time and a lot of love and patience on parents' behalf for this fear to disappear. Consider the drawings 4.1, 4.2, 4.3, and 4.4. The themes of anxiety and a need for reassurance that their new families love them are present in each drawing. Each picture has a tree, clinging closely to the house. To these children, the trees represent themselves, while the houses represent their new environments. Interestingly enough, the adoptive parents do not usually appear on the drawings, while the house tends to be the central object. This is indicative of the cognitive processes of formulating new schema, related to the new surroundings that these children are placed into. Their new homes become symbols of the new lives. Having concrete, positive imagery of the new house helps these children to accommodate to a new life. The houses, often the central objects of the drawings, tend to be big, with many windows that represent the openness toward new experiences (4.1, 4.4). The windows are usually well lit with warm yellow light, that reflects the warmth and loving that these children are receiving from their new families (4.2, 4.4). Persistent anxiety that the new life is just a passing dream, makes these children want to attach themselves as closely to their new homes as they can. The trees are drawn close to the houses (4.1, 4.2, and 4.3) and are well grounded, which is symbolic of the children's growing roots in their new environments.

Overall, these pictures tend to be colorful and full of hope, sun is present in most of the pictures and is shining bright onto the homes (new family) and the trees (the children themselves).

Samples of drawings from children whose adoption occurred longer ago, allowing more time to adjust to their new environment, show a different pattern. These children are more confident that they are loved and accepted by their new families, and feel.assured that they will not be sent back to foster homes even if they misbehave. Their anxieties have diminished, allowing these children to experience more positive feelings (joy, happiness, etc.). Although trees are still sometimes present in the pictures, they are now more detached from the houses (4.5). The houses tend to be drawn smaller, and are not necessarily placed in the center of the picture (4.5, 4.7). Because these youngsters have come to trust their parents' love for them, and do not crave a constant proof of the parents' affection, there is less emphasis on well-let windows (4.6, 4.8). These children feel safer than the first group, and they express it by placing some distance between their homes and themselves in their drawings. They are now able to separate from their new adoptive families and are emotionally ready to meet the world that is waiting outside the house walls. An appearance of objects other than houses and trees also signifies the children's ability to expand their horizons and focus on interests other than their new family (4.7). To allow a space for new experiences, these children's' drawings are less clustered (4.5, 4.7).

Overall, the drawings of the children who have been living with their new families for a longer time than the above group tend to be brighter, sunnier, and more spacious with happier themes emerging.

The implications of understanding the patterns of drawings by adopted children are far-reaching. A sensitive counselor should be attuned towards the changes in the drawings,

Chapter 4

them in the therapy process. For many children, drawing serves as a tool to express the feelings that are difficult to articulate verbally. For adopted children, who do not speak the language of their new country, art therapy offers a unique opportunity for communication.

There is much more to say about the art therapy with adaptive families. This chapter had touched upon 'the tip of the iceberg'. One of the books in this series will be dedicated to art therapy with adopted children.

Appendix

	TOPIC	ADJUSTMENT			ANXIETY			DEPRESSION			POST-TRAUMATIC			TOTAL	%OF TOTAL
		1	*2*	*3*	*4*	*5*	*6*	*7*	*8*	*9*	*10*	*11*	*12*		
#1	FLOWERS	9.2	8	15.1	12.3	13	24.5	19.2	19	35.8	17.3	13	24.5	53	14.4
#2	WATER/SUN/MOON	8.0	7	24.1	7.5	8	27.6	8.1	8	27.6	8.0	6	20.7	29	7.9
#3	NATURE	10.3	9	24.3	8.5	9	24.3	10.1	10	27.0	12.0	9	24.3	37	10.1
#4	LIFE	6.9	6	23.1	7.5	8	30.8	8.1	8	30.8	5.3	4	15.4	26	7.1
#5	PEOPLE	21.8	19	37.3	11.3	12	23.5	9.1	9	17.6	14.7	11	21.6	51	13.9
#6	ANIMALS	5.7	5	35.7	2.8	3	21.4	2.0	2	14.3	5.3	4	28.6	14	3.8
#7	ABSTRACT	20.7	18	17.3	36.8	39	37.5	30.3	30	28.8	22.7	17	16.3	104	28.3
#8	WORDS	8.0	7	30.4	4.7	5	21.7	7.1	7	30.4	5.3	4	17.4	23	6.3
#9	STILL LIFE/COLLAGES	9.2	8	26.7	8.5	9	30.0	6.1	6	20.0	9.3	7	23.3	30	8.2
	TOTAL	100	87		100	106		100	99		100	75		367	100.0
	%OF TOTAL	23.7			28.9			27.0			20.4			100.0	

NOTES:

Column #1 - percent of each particular theme within all paintings by people with adjustment disorder.

Column #2 - amount of paintings of each theme by people with adjustment disorder

Column #3 - percent of paintings by people with adjustment disorder within a given theme

Column #4 - percent of each particular theme within all paintings by people with anxiety

Column #5 - amount of paintings of each theme by people with anxiety

Column #6 - percent of paintings by people with anxiety within a given theme

Column #7 - percent of each particular theme within all paintings by people with depression

Column #8 - amount of paintings of each theme by people with depression

Column #9 - percent of paintings by people with depression within a given theme

Column #10 - amount of paintings of each particular theme within all paintings by people with post-traumatic stress disorder

Column #11 - amount of paintings of each theme by people with post-traumatic stress disorder

Column #12 - percent of paintings by people with post-traumatic stress disorder within a given theme

ABSTRACT	PLATES	WORDS	STILL LIFE/COLLAGES	TOTALS
ANXIETY		ADJUSTMENT,DEPRESSION	ANXIETY	ANXIETY
DEPRESSION		ANXIETY	ADJUSTMENT	DEPRESSION
ADJUSTMENT		POST-TRAUMATIC	POST-TRAUMATIC	ADJUSTMENT
POST-TRAUMATIC			DEPRESSION	POST-TRAUMATIC

	FLOWERS	WATER/SUN/MOON	NATURE	LIFE	PEOPLE	ANIMALS
MOST	DEPRESSION	ANXIETY, DEPRESSION	DEPRESSION	ANXIETY,DEPRESSION	ADJUSTMENT	ADJUSTME
	ANXIETY, POST-TRAUMATIC	ADJUSTMENT	ADJUSTMENT,ANXIETY,POST-TRAUMATIC	ADJUSTMENT	ANXIETY	POST-TRA
	ADJUSMENT	POST-TRAUMATIC		POST-TRAUMATIC	POST-TRAUMATIC	ANXIETY
LEAST					DEPRESSION	DEPRESSIO

Index of Pictorial

Using this table you can have a quick reference for a special
picture fig ures you interested in.

Research Data

Of almost 4000 paintings analyzed, 367 were chosen for their typicality to represent this body of art works. There are 87 paintings by people with Adjustment disorder, 106 paintings by people with Anxiety disorder, 99 paintings by people with Depression, and 75 paintings by people with Post-Traumatic Stress disorder. The paintings are organized into nine categories: flowers, water/sun/moon, nature, city life, people, animals, abstract, words, and still life/collages. Almost a third of all the paintings (104) are abstract. Other "popular" themes include flowers (almost 16.6% of all paintings), and people and nature (each about 10% of total). Least popular themes are words (6.3% of total) and animals of total).

Bibliography

Altman, C.H. (1960). projective techniques in the clinical setting. In A. I. Rabine & M. R. Haworth (Eds.), Projective techniques with children. New York: Grune & Stratton.

Apfeldorf, M., & Smith, W. (1966). The presentation of the body self in human figure drawings. Journal of Projective Techniques and Personality Assessment, 30, 283-289.

Barnes, E. (1892). A study of children's drawings. Pedagogical Seminary, 2, 455-463.

Bjolgerud, E. (1977). Children's view of the parent's roles in home and society as shown in their drawings. Master's thesis, University of Oslo.

Blount, C. (1981). Changing family roles. Ph.D. dissertation. Seattle University.

Britain, F. L. (1970). Effects of manipulation of children's affect on their family draw ings. *Journal of Projective Techniques and Personality Assessments*, 34, 324-327.

Brown, T. R. (1977). KFD in evaluating foster home care. Office of Research, State of Washington, Dept. of Social and Health Services. Olympia, WA.

Burns, R. C. (1980). What children are telling us in their human figure drawings. *Early Childhood Council*, 11, 3. Saskatchewan, Canada.

Cummings, J. A. (1982, August). Research on projective drawings: Implications for practice. Paper presented at the annual meeting of the American psychological Association, Washington, D.C.

Dileo, J. H. (1973). *Children's Drawings as Diagnostic Aids.* Brunner?Mazel, New York.

Exner, J. E. (1976). In I. B. Weiner (Ed.), Clinical methods in psychology (pp. 61-121). New York: Wiley

Falk, J. D. (1981). Understanding children's art: An analysis of the literature. Journal of Personality Assessment, 33, 409-413.

Freeman, H. (July, !971). What a child's drawings can reveal. *Mother*, 35, 34-36. London.

Hall, C. S, & Lindzey, G. (1978). Theories of personality (3rd. ed.). New York: Wiley.

Holtzberg, J. D. (1968). Psychological theory and projective techniques. In A. I. Rabin (Ed.), Projective techniques in personality assessment. New York: Springer.

Hulse, W. C. (1951). The emotionally disturbed child draws his family. *Quarterly Journal of Child Behavior.* 3:152-174.

Jung, C. G. (1979). *Word and Image.* Bollingen Series XCVLL. Princeton, N.J.: Princeton Univ. Press.

Kato, T. (1979). Pictorial expression of family relations in young children. 1X International Congress of Psychopathology of Expression. Verona, Italy.

Klepsch, M. & Logie, L. (1982). *Children Draw and Tell. Brunner/Mazel,* New York.

Knoff, H. M. & Prout, H. (1985). *The Kinetic Drawing System - Family and School: A Handbook.* Los Angeles. Western Psychological Services.

Koppitz, E. M. (1968). *Psychological Evaluation of Children's Human Figure Drawing.* Grune and Stratton. New York.

Lanyon, R. I., & Goodstein, D. (1981). the future of clinical assessment. American Psychologist, 36, 1147-1158.

Leary, T. F. (1957). The interpersonal diagnosis of personality. New York: Ronald Press.

Machover, K. (1949). *Personality Projection in the Drawing of the Human Figure.* Springfield IL: Charles C Thomas.

McDonald, M. (1980). Relationship between father/daughter incest as manifest in K-F-Ds of adolescent girls. Thesis: Antioch University, San Francisco.

Mentor, J. (1981). Values clarification through art forms: A projective technique. M. A. thesis, San Francisco Theological Seminary.

Metzner, R. (Fall, 1957). The tree as a symbol of self unfoldment. *The American Theosophist.*

Murstein, B. I. (1963). Theory and research in projective techniques. New York: Wiley.

Prout, H. T. & Celmer, D. S. (1984). School drawings and academic achiecement: A validity study of the kinetic school drawing technique. *Psychology in the Schools*, 21, 176-180.

Puryear, D. L. (1984). Familial experiences: A comparison between the children of les bian mothers and the children of heterosexual mothers. Dissertation Abstracts International. 44, 3941B. University Microfilms No. 84-03, 829.

Rogers, C. R. (1963). *On Becoming a Person.* Boston: Houghton Mifflen.

Sobel, M. & Sobel, W.(1976). Discriminating adolescent male delinquents through the use of kinetic family drawings. *Journal of Personality Assessment*, 40, 91-94.